“The connector's bi … get
with every page. If … ps,
your network, or you … ake
you to growth you've never dreamed possible.”

—Michael J. Maher, bestselling author of *(7L) The Seven Levels of Communication: Go from Relationships to Referrals and The Miracle Morning for Real Estate Agents,* and founder of The Generosity Generation.

“*Your Connecting Advantage* is the definitive book on effectively establishing your personal brand, increasing your encounters for real results and maximizing your accessibility using current technology in combination with valuable business networking events. More than just another “how to network” book, Joyce's latest book is a blueprint to connecting strategically, building a lasting network and creating lucrative relationships online and off. Whether you are in direct sales, working inside a corporation or just striking out on your own, this book is your ticket to fast-tracking your business success.”

—Ray Robbins, Mannatech Co-Founder

“From the minute I met Joyce, I knew she was an amazing! And *Your Connecting Advantage* is just as remarkable. Life is ultimately about connections and relationships. She has marvelously created a platform for anyone, beginners or seasoned veterans, to utilize this book as a path to success.”

—Johnna Beckham, Founder|CEO of JOHNNA MARIE: custom clothing for women

"Success tactics to turn life into one big connecting opportunity!" What a great quote from such an insightful and powerful writer. Joyce Layman brings compelling inspiration into the realm of what makes *Your Connecting Advantage* set you apart in the land of look-a-likes. People want to stand out…be heard…be recognized and remembered for who they are and how they help others. Joyce offers us the opportunity to leverage relationships by connecting on a level that will result in the outcomes we want. The slight turn of the phrase from networking to the use of the word connecting is a powerful statement. This is a joy to read and lessons to be learned for a lifetime. If you want more in your personal and business life…read this book now! Pass it on to others and let's connect!"

—Linda K. Nottberg-Endecott, Partner, iValution

"In *Your Connecting Advantage,* Joyce Layman takes the art of genuine relationship building and combines it with the science of strategic connecting. Her book could not have come at a better time for me as I am repurposing my personal brand from the football field to the corporate world. I look forward to incorporating more of her connecting principles and watching my influence grow."

—Jon McGraw, Principal at Vision Pursue &
10-year veteran of the NFL

YOUR CONNECTING ADVANTAGE

Success tactics to turn life into one big ~~networking~~ connecting opportunity

Joyce Layman

BOOSTING PERSONAL BRAND,
AMPLIFYING INFLUENCE &
ENHANCING STRATEGIC RELATIONSHIPS

Your Connecting Advantage

Success Tactics to Turn Life Into One Big ~~Networking~~
Connecting Opportunity

ISBN 978-1515115748
Published by
JL Enterprises LLC
Kansas City, MO
U.S.A.
Cover and Interior Design by: Jun Ares

To order additional copies, visit www.JoyceLayman.com

"For all those who know that giving is worth more than receiving and who believe in investing their time to create meaningful relationships... this book is for you."

CONTENTS

ACKNOWLEDGMENTS

If I were to acknowledge individually all the people who helped make *Your Connecting Advantage* possible, at least nine more chapters would be necessary.

I want to thank Jennifer for pushing me out of my book writing comfort zone (twice), getting the plan together (then working it), and helping me maintain sanity and sense of humor along the way. Here's to friendship, coffee, and wine!

To those who sent me an abundance of energy, insight, and love. Everything worked out perfectly…of course!

Thank you to my island alliances. I said it once, but it's well worth repeating: you exemplify the true meaning of super-connectors, and I'd trust you with my proxy anytime!

To the influencers who welcomed me into your networks: for that, I am grateful.

Thanks to my family. You always have and always will be my rock. I love you.

To my professional team: Erin, thank you for taking my words and putting your special touch of magic on them. Thank you, Ares, for your masterful creation of the cover and interior design. And thanks to Lea for the caret.

And to those who think a story in the book is about you, you're probably right. Thanks for being the inspiration.

INTRODUCTION

What's the first thing that comes to mind when you hear the word "networking"? Do you immediately recall a great event where you made some stellar connections, or do you recall an event that left you thinking "I'd rather shoot myself than ever show up at one of those again"? Too often networking conjures an image of shallow events where strangers gather together for small talk and exchange business cards, hoping to sell each other. The event itself isn't the problem; it's the expectations that far too many people have of what they are supposed to do at a networking event that are the problem.

Maybe you've been on the receiving end of a card counter who thinks the number of business cards they collect equals the size of their network? And then there are those times when you have an enjoyable conversation and exchange cards with someone who says, "I'd love to meet for coffee," but then that person magically enters the witness protection program for bad networkers.

Do a Google search for business networking and you'll find 134,000,000 results. The information tends to follow the same path: meet someone, exchange cards, follow up to expand your network, and repeat. But only a small percentage emphasizes that networking is really about creating meaningful relationships with individuals who share the same philosophy. If your desire is to experience quality conversations and mutually beneficial connections, you'll be pleased to know that *Your Connecting Advantage* takes networking out of the equation. Unless you're living in a cave or under a rock, you're already connecting with people on a daily basis. That could be at work, via social media, at your kid's soccer game, over a business lunch, or even out running. It's what you do with those interactions that counts and it starts with the small details.

Focusing on making connections without giving a lot of thought to your personal brand could be costing you opportunities and business.

What impression do people get when they Google you? Your personal brand and social capital are more important now than ever before, and that's where the book starts. You've probably heard the old adage that it takes seven seconds to make an impression. Research shows it's actually one-tenth of a second, and misperceptions take far longer to correct if you even get the chance to do it. Whether you're just entering the business world or have been in the workforce for years, your personal brand is essential for creating your connecting advantage. If you don't know where to start, you can waste a lot of time and money. I should know, as I invested over $23,000 doing the wrong things to establish my brand when I first launched my business.

Once your brand is in place, it's time to get crystal-clear about the value you provide and then to be able to translate it in a way that inspires and motivates others to want to connect with you. We go past typical marketing-speak to help you discover what makes you stand out in a sea of vanilla. Your best connections can happen at any time, so preparation is key.

Did you know we are internally hardwired to resist change? It's what kept us alive in hunter-gatherer days. For the introverts, it keeps them stuck at their desks instead of facing a group of strangers. Internal comfort zones and head trash can also keep you from pursuing new connections and making that critical ask. You'll gain insight here about how the mind works at the conscious and—more importantly—subconscious levels. The information will also help you to hone your mental filter and to see new connecting opportunities that already surround you. The bonus is being able to apply these same concepts in other areas of your life.

You'll also gain insights for increasing your "collision rates" and creating serendipitous encounters. Endlessly surfing the internet won't lead to the connections you're looking for unless you have a strategy in place to find them and develop the relationships. In case you weren't already aware, coffee shops are the new business hot spot.

Being intentional about your meetings can turn a typical one-on-one meeting into nine connections in two hours. Your best connection could be the person in the office next to you but if you haven't told them who you're looking to meet, it's another missed connection.

In case you're wondering, in this book, there's actually an entire chapter devoted to maximizing opportunities at networking events as well as conferences and even while "sweatworking." Whether you're new to relationship development or looking to expand your current network, you'll learn about how to determine the best places to make connections for your business and your goals. This chapter also includes brilliant conversation starters, body language tips, a caution about the cost of judging, guidance about mastering the art of social jiujitsu, and more.

Making a new connection doesn't mean anything unless you follow up. If you're not quite sure about what to write in a follow-up email or note, examples are included. You'll find tactics to simplify the prioritizing and managing of relationships. For those of you who want to further the connection online, customized invitations to connect on LinkedIn are included, too.

Did you know that you can create serendipity for others with a little planning? Your intent will determine if a connecting happy hour, mastermind dinner, strategic roundtable, or adventure (to name a few) is the best strategy. And then there are opportunities to facilitate an introduction between two people in your network. How you do it speaks volumes and also affects how you receive introductions from others.

Whether offline or online, there are numerous ways to add value to those in your network. When done correctly, you'll increase your influence and expand your social capital. Developing new relationships takes time and so does adding value to existing relationships. Simple steps form trusted alliances with people who are motivated to help each other out. In this book, you'll learn ways to teach others how they can recognize business opportunities or resources that would be of benefit to you and know how to spot a terrific opportunity for them as well.

If you don't have a strategy in place and clear idea of the people that you want to meet, you could easily miss recognizing that the person standing next to you could be a valuable addition to your network. It's time to stop connecting by accident or assuming that connections will fall into your lap.

Your Connecting Advantage will help you learn how to weed out those people who are only in it to take. And if you need to fire a client or end a relationship with an energy vampire, you'll gain insight about when and how to handle the breakup process. These are just a few of the things you'll find inside. Each chapter builds on the next and includes real-world examples, ideas, and tactics that you can apply to your connecting strategy along with the research to validate key concepts. You'll also have access to the latest #connectinghacks in the book and on my website, too. Even if you have a love-hate relationship with technology, you'll find value with these hacks.

Four of the most dangerous words in the English language are, "I already know that." You can intellectualize it and talk about it, but unless you're taking action, it doesn't count for much. You are most likely doing some of the things discussed in the book but may not have considered how they work together. *Your Connecting Advantage* helps you create a strategy that fits with your goals and personal style. There are tactics here that work with your strengths, regardless of whether you're an introvert, ambivert, extrovert, new to building a network, or a seasoned connector. The concepts apply to those who are just launching a business, shifting careers, high school students, recent college grads, people in business development, CEO's, super-connectors, and everyone in between.

To see me now, you'd think I was born a natural networker. In fact, that's the furthest thing from the truth, and I was really bad at it at first. If you are a TEDx fan and care to see how someone was able to shift from a wallflower to a connector, my TEDx talk shares the 15 minute version of my story.

My journey started when I attended training in The Pacific Institute's processes. I added The Pacific Institute's training to my experience in sales and consulting to launch my own business. At the same time that I was helping my clients navigate challenges and create change in their businesses, I was doing the same in my own. Social media was just taking off, and the power of a personal brand wasn't even on my radar.

The learning curve took years, but once I understood the strategy that worked for me and the right actions to take, I started making amazing connections with people like Bob Burg. You'll read in the book that when I was stumbling through networking, it was his book *Endless Referrals* that lit my path. The combination of shifting my belief of what was possible, pushing my own comfort zones and expanding my network started to create incredible results that surprised me. I knew I was on the right track and that gave me the confidence to set even bolder goals. Bob graciously endorsed my first book, *Just Another Leap*, and referred to me as the greatest networker in the world. Others that I hold in high regard have said the same thing, which is very humbling. My reply: "I learned from the best."

To me, a networker is someone who connects to people as well as connects people to people. Being a connector is more than connecting people to people; it's also connecting people to ideas and resources. My intent is to share with you the knowledge I've gained as well as to give insight about the connections you need to make and to open your eyes to the ones who are ideal whom you haven't even considered...yet.

I don't feel the need to reinvent the wheel or attempt to be everything to everyone. In the process of researching the book, I was fortunate to come across a number of experts with content and assessments that was relevant to specific sections in the book. It's easy to find a plethora of "experts" with different specialties, but I was looking for the experts to the experts. William Arruda, Dorie Clark, Bob Burg, Daniel Pink, Jeff Haden, Cameron Herold, Jayson Gaignard, and Adam Grant have all graciously agreed to let me share their wisdom with you. In order to keep the book from turning into a trilogy, I only shared a small portion of what they have to offer. You'll find their website, social media links and contact information at the back of the book. If you're not familiar their work, I highly suggest you add them to your knowledge list.

To get the most out of the book, I'd suggest reading it front-to-back, as the concepts in each chapter build on each other. Key references are included, and the content might not connect if you missed the introduction of a person or idea. You'll find examples that you can easily apply to wherever you are at in your connecting development. If you think everything in this book is something you've never heard before, well that's just not true. However, according to folks in my network, there are a few examples that even surprised them and will probably leave you wondering, "How did she think of that?"

Good news: no quizzes, but you will find action steps at the end of each chapter to help you develop your own connecting advantage strategy. There are three action steps at the end of each chapter, and you'll decide the specific steps you need to work on according to what you feel are most important to your strategy right now. If you're the type of person who likes to take notes in the margin of the book or highlight text with your Kindle, then be sure to do that as you go along. It will save you time when you get to the end of the chapter. You could easily have nineteen things that you feel you need to do or want to accomplish, and that's great. To stay focused and not be overwhelmed, you'll pick the top three for now. The steps are delineated by time. For example, your Fast Start action steps—which include things like updating your contact information on a social media platform—will take you fifteen minutes or fewer. Your One-Hour Win steps will take up to an hour, and the third Snail It steps will require more time, like setting up a meeting with a connection or hosting a gathering.

The action steps aren't just something to do for the heck of it. They can actually generate a return for the time you invest in doing them as long as they are aligned with your connecting strategy. You may get to chapter five, have an epiphany, and want to tweak your strategy. Nothing is set in stone, so do it. The intention of the book is to give you as much information as possible so you can create what works best for you.

As a mindset shifter with a knack for pushing clients' comfort zones, I know that some of the examples in the book just might upset your networking apple cart. The good news is that I'll give you strategies, tactics, and even some new apples to work with.

My promise to you as you read the book is that if you have any questions, would like clarification, are uncertain about a particular tactic or would even like to share a strategy that's worked for you, by all means let me know. You can do this via social media through Facebook.com/joycelaymanfan or Twitter.com/joycelayman. Of course, email is always an option. I make the offer every time I'm in front of an audience and wanted to extend it to my readers as well so please ask away.

I look forward to connecting with you.

Now, onto chapter one!

CHAPTER 1

FIRST IMPRESSIONS, SOCIAL CAPITAL AND VANILLA SEAS

FIRST IMPRESSIONS

Why start with personal branding when this is a book about creating your connecting advantage? First, let's get clear about the intent for building a personal brand. In an article written for *Fast Company* in 1997, business branding and management expert Tom Peters writes, "Today brands are everything, and all kinds of products and services—from accounting firms to sneaker makers to restaurants—are figuring out how to transcend the narrow boundaries of their categories and become a brand surrounded by a Tommy Hilfiger-like buzz."

Tom goes on, explaining that "Regardless of age, regardless of position, regardless of the business we happen to be in, all of us need to understand the importance of branding. We are CEOs of our own companies: Me Inc. To be in business today, our most important job is to be head marketer for the brand called You."

Peters wasn't the first to mention the term *personal branding*. In 1937, Napoleon Hill mentioned "self-positioning" in his book *Think and Grow Rich*. Today, personal branding has reached a new level of importance thanks to the growth of the virtual world. It's hard to deny that your personal brand is intertwined with your business and what you do in off-hours.

A powerful personal brand has everything to do with connecting because your brand could be the first experience that someone has with you. A potential client might look you up online. Or someone you're introduced to through email might check out your LinkedIn profile. Or one of your strategic partners might give your business card to a new contact. In each of these situations, your personal brand is absolutely critical, whether your goal is to sell a product, build a business, attain another position within your current company, find a new opportunity, or become a thought leader in your industry. Wherever you go and whatever you do, your brand influences how you connect.

When someone looks at your online profile, as harsh as it may sound, do they see somebody worth connecting to? More importantly, have you earned the right to tell the story of You? What I mean by that is, have you done the work? If you call yourself an expert, have you lived what you are selling? You can position yourself as an expert on YouTube and other social media platforms and gain followers, but does that mean you know your stuff?

A personal brand is about taking a proactive approach to create and manage perceptions and conversations about you in person and online.

A personal brand isn't about creating a false representation of who you are, what you do, and what you're capable of. Between the power of the internet, social media platforms, and one or two degrees of separation (we'll cover more about that concept soon), you're going to be found out eventually. The fallout after the hacking of Ashley Madison data is just one instance of how this has proved to be true.

Creating a personal brand starts with a strategy. Otherwise, you can waste time and money in the wrong places.

AN ACCIDENTIAL BRAND?

For me, creating my personal brand was a very backward thing. I didn't create online profiles based on where I was in my career at that time. I did it because I thought it was the thing to do. I made a guest appearance on MySpace, but that was about it. LinkedIn was just for a job search, right? Facebook was easy enough to navigate, and I looked at it simply as a way to connect with friends and family. Then there was Twitter. How on Earth can you communicate successfully with just 140 characters? It was a bit confusing. The only reason I created a profile was so that I could follow a cycling group in Kansas City. Thankfully, I was smart enough to go grab my name as my Twitter handle, **@joycelayman**.

But the point is that I wasn't thinking about how these online profiles were going to be part of my personal brand. I was building my personal brand by accident, without any thought to long-range strategy.

I hired a company to build a website and paid a small fortune for it. I invested in trade marking to protect my company brand. There was also the expense of logo development and printed materials for marketing. By the time all was said and done, I had spent over $23,000 on building my company brand. But most of that expense wasn't necessary. Now, that's not to say that the people I worked with didn't have the right skillset. They were really good at what they did, and that's why I hired them.

But, looking back, I realize that no one asked how my personal brand would evolve as my business did. My social media profiles are under the name "Joyce Layman," yet the company name on my website and my business cards was "Mind By Design." There was a disconnect because when someone introduced me before a keynote presentation or at a meeting, it was as Joyce Layman, not as Joyce Layman with Mind By Design. People only knew my name, not the name of my business.

What I didn't realize was that it was the brand of myself that was more important than a company name since I was building my business as a keynote speaker and consultant. Ultimately, I wasted a lot of time and spent a lot of money because I didn't step back to look at the big picture. My strategy seemed to be the result of shiny-object syndrome: whenever I met someone whom I could hire to help me build my business and market it, I dove in. At that time, I was more focused on marketing the business Mind by Design. But very little of that was necessary for brand Joyce.

ONLINE, OFFLINE, SIDELINED

At one time, all you heard about were company brands. A company brand is critical for a large organizations and startups alike. It's a fantastic achievement when a company comes into its own as an easily recognizable brand. Personal branding started to gain notoriety when William Arruda founded Reach Personal Branding in 2001. After working for over 20 years in branding and in consulting for three Fortune 500 companies as well as launching the first personal brand assessment—which has been used by nearly one-million professionals and entrepreneurs—William is considered a branding expert.

Today personal branding is a household term. As someone working within a company, no matter if—or *especially* if—you are the business owner, you need to have not just a company brand but your personal brand as well. Consider how the two brands support each other. Even if you're currently working for someone else, your personal brand is critical because it represents your effort, your ability, and your skillset. Maybe you volunteer for a particular non-profit or sit on a board, or you're part of a cycling group or a running group or have another hobby that you spend a lot of time at. Your personal brand is going to support you wherever you're at in your career in a way that's different from your company brand. The odds are that you won't be in the same position with the same company for the rest of your career, especially if you're part of the millennial generation. *Forbes*' Jeanne Meister reports that the average worker stays in a job between four and five years, while many millennials plan to change jobs every three years, which means they might have as many as 20 jobs by the time they retire. The only consistent thing during all that job hopping is your personal brand.

The goal is for your personal brand to be the most accurate representation of who you are and what you're capable of. A study by the executive search firm ExecuNet found that 77 percent of recruiters run searches on the web to screen applicants, and 35 percent say they have eliminated a candidate based on the information they uncovered. If you're in a company and you're trying to move from one department to another, your online presence—especially your LinkedIn profile—is key. And if you're looking at changing careers or moving out of one niche or one industry into another, you want to be in the best possible position to land the right job as quickly as possible.

EXPECTATIONS AND BRAND PERCEPTION

Gary Vaynerchuk, author of *Crush It!*, says, "It's important to build a personal brand because it's the only thing you're going to have. Your reputation online, and in the new business world is pretty much the game, so you've got to be a good person. You can't hide anything, and more importantly, you've got to be out there at some level."

You can pay a company to create your brand, or you can do it yourself. No matter what, it isn't an overnight process. Your personal brand should set expectations about who you are in person as well as in the virtual world. You can use your personal brand to highlight those aspects of yourself that speak to what is valued within an organization as well as within your own network.

If you don't control your brand, somebody else can. You may be the best at what you do, but how others perceive you is just as important. This goes for in-person interactions as well as online. People may not take the time to get to know you if they don't see a reason to. Judgments—whether right or wrong—are still made.

What do people think when they hear your name? When somebody says, "I want to introduce you to Joyce Layman," for example, what do you think is the first thought that comes to mind? You may be familiar with the phrase "six degrees of separation." Depending on the city you live in, you could easily be just one or two degrees away from your next valuable connection. Whether in person or online, if you are not projecting the right image, then your obstacle will be overcoming who others perceive you to be. A powerful personal brand is a key step to creating your connecting advantage.

JUST GO GOOGLE YOURSELF

The first thing that you need to do to assess your personal brand is to search for yourself on Google. What shows up and, more importantly, is it accurate? Do this in multiple browsers because information will show up differently depending on whether you're using Safari, Chrome, or another browser. The same results may also show up in different orders in different browsers. Be sure to look at six or seven pages of search results to make sure that you're seeing the full extent of information that's out there.

Be sure to search Google images, too. If you've been tagged in photos—whether on a website, in a newspaper article, or at special event—and your name is tagged or associated with those images online, those photos will show up in your Google image search.

From your Google search, make a list of the content, profiles, and images you found that need to be updated, changed, or even deleted. Once you make the change, it can take weeks or even months for the Google search results to change.

The next step is to measure how your personal brand stacks up on the world wide web. You can do this for free with the Online ID Calculator designed by William Arruda.

www.onlineidcalculator.com

The Online ID Calculator measures the volume and relevance of your name search results. In addition, it also measures purity, diversity and validation. According to the Calculator web page, your Purity score speaks to how many of the search results are about you, not someone else. It will show you how well you've done building relevant, high ranking content. Diversity measures the amount of relevant images and videos you've posted. These could be on Twitter, YouTube, and more. Building a brand involves being both visible and credible. When your online profiles contain feedback from other people, it enhances your Validation measurement. Feedback in the form of recommendations, gives the people who are researching you a chance to learn more about you from other's experiences with you.

If you'd like to know how others perceive your brand, consider the 360Reach personal brand survey. The survey gives you the ability to obtain feedback from clients, colleagues, employees, professors, family, friends, etc. You can find more details about it on the ReachCC.com website.

TOO MANY BOB JONES

The kicker is that you can't always control whether somebody else has the same name as yours and what they are posting. If what they're posting isn't something you want associated with your personal brand, you may have extra work involved to improve your search engine rankings and change what people see when they search for your name. In some extreme cases, it may take an attorney to resolve the problem. But the extra work will be worth it. Your personal brand is a *big* deal.

Let me tell you two stories that explain just how important controlling your personal brand online is.

I came across a professional speaker who had the same name as a porn star. Needless to say, that wasn't an accurate representation of this person's brand. When somebody—like a potential client—searched for this person on Google, guess who had the advantage in the search engine optimization or SEO department? It would take not just time but a ton of cash to take over the top rankings. In this case, the professional speaker couldn't remove anything that was posted by the other person. All that could be done was to enhance the brand that the speaker had created.

When I first started building my business back in 2008, there was a real estate agent on the East Coast with the same name. Since then, I've managed to take over the first two pages and most of the third page of Google search results. The results show my websites, social media profiles, TEDxUMKC video, Amazon.com link to my books, speakers bureau bios, and more. With all the websites, posting content and making sure profiles are updated as changes are made is a regular activity. All that being said, you have control over anything that you post online, even if you don't necessarily have control over what someone else posts online in your name. You can always hire a company to clean up what you can't change on your own, but you'll have to consider how much of an investment you want to make in that clean-up. One of the best things you can do is to set up alerts about new online content associated with your name. Google used to have service called Google Alerts that could let you know if new search results became available for a specific search phrase (like your name or your company's name), but since they recently changed the algorithms, it's not really the best tool for being alerted to specific, new online content anymore.

#CONNECTINGHACK

Talkwalker Alerts is one of several free services that provides alerts like Google Alerts.

Considering how quickly things change, it would be impossible to list every hack in Your Connecting Advantage. That would be a full time job in itself. There are a number of #hacks in the resource section of the book, and you can also find the most up-to-date list on my website by going to:

www.yourconnectingadvantage.com/connectinghacks

THE TALE OF TWO NAMES

When it comes to online personal branding, women have an additional issue to consider: their last names. Have you had a name change, or is one on the horizon? This can be a bit perplexing for people who are trying to find you or learn more about you online, so consider the name that people will most likely use in a search to find you.

I had a name change several years ago, and instead of making a complete switch, I chose to add on my new last name with a hyphen. I'm represented on the websites of numerous speakers' bureaus, and when I later wanted to remove the hyphenated portion of my name, it took time to get my name changed on those websites and to get URLs updated. There's still one listing that I can't get resolved. No matter how many emails or tweets, I have yet to get the site managers to respond. It appears they aren't paying attention to their Twitter feed and don't value good customer service.

You'll need to consider how you want to take ownership of your online space in terms of what name you want to be associated with that space. Think about how you might manage a transition if a change in your relationship status affects your name.

The other thing to consider—no matter if you're a man or woman—is misspellings. If you have a name that could easily be spelled two ways like mine—Layman or Laymen—you'll want to purchase the domain for both versions. Redirect the domain name with the incorrect spelling to your actual website so folks will find you when doing a search.

You can also include the versions of your name in your LinkedIn profile. Branding expert William Arruda has done just that in his profile: AKA/Misspellings: Bill Arruda, William Aruda.

YOUR NAME...NOT YOUR SPACE

Your bio on your company's website—whether your own your company or you work for someone else—is another important part of this equation. Is your information in that bio consistent with the brand you want? Does it all reflect you in the right way? Consistency is key.

If you own a company, what does the company website say about you? Is the brand of the company consistent with what you want it to be? According to research by Google and CEB's Marketing Leadership Council, 57 percent of customers' purchases are completed online before they choose to do business with your company. Even if you aren't that tech-savvy, know that others are, and they do online searches. With all the competition your business faces, first impressions are critical. So once again, if your information isn't accurate, up-to-date, focused on your target audience, and speaking to their pain or their problem, then you could be losing customers or potential connections.

BUT THAT'S MY NAME

Domains are a critical part of the personal brand strategy. I am very grateful to the guy who bought my domain when I didn't have a clue about how important it would be in my career. His name is Michael Maher. When we first met, Michael was a real estate agent in Kansas City. He's now considered North America's most referred real estate professional and author of the bestselling book (7L) The Seven Levels of Communication: Go from Relationships to Referrals.

Michael was also a marketing genius and knew the value of building a brand. At the time, I was an associate for a company that did training. Michael and I were introduced at a networking event. We scheduled coffee, and after that meeting, he sent an email that said, "I bought JoyceLayman.com for you." Since I was working for someone else, I didn't realize what a gift Michael was giving me. But now I do. When I started getting strategic about building my own brand, I saw the domain's value, and I launched my own business out of it. So, never say never to getting your own domain because you don't always know where your career path may lead.

A few years ago, I was meeting with a real estate broker, and I brought up the question, "Have you Googled yourself, and do you own your own domain name?" He replied, "When you Google me, you'll find lots of things related to real estate." And I said, "What about your personal domain?" He said, "Well, it isn't that important."

My curiosity got the best of me, so I suggested doing a quick search on GoDaddy to see if his name was available to be purchased as a domain (sidenote: there are a lot of sites that allow you to search for a specific domain name and then, if the domain is available, purchase that domain from them) and found out that his name had already been purchased. This was surprising because his name has a very unusual spelling. I went to Whois to look up who owned the domain. It just so happens that it was the real estate agent's ex-business partner, and they hadn't parted ways on good terms. The domain redirected users to a different website. Let's just say the other website was as far removed as possible from the interests of this man, who is married with children. And that's not to say it's a bad website, but it certainly wasn't consistent with his brand. To get his name back as his domain, he'll most likely to have to pay thousands of dollars and hire an attorney.

Now parents, especially parents of young children, consider what's going on with personal branding of the millennial generation and how common it is today for people to switch industries. In 2007,

GoDaddy's president of registration, Warren Adelman, said that domains are "the foundation upon which all the other Internet services are based." *Forbes* suggests parents should look up their children's names to see if they're available as domains because "Claiming a name online today is growing harder and harder as available URL's keep disappearing." You don't know what they'll want to do as a career, especially if each of them has as many as 20 jobs before retiring. And if they're in a creative field or they start their own companies, having the domain name that they want is going to be even more critical. It's certainly worth an investment of the typical fee for purchasing a domain, which is about $13 a year. So don't wait to look up your kids' names and see if you can purchase a domain with their name. Do it now.

Millennial or not, let's consider just one example of how important domain names are in relation to one's personal brand. Taylor Swift is a well-known singer, and she has managed to dominate when it comes to claiming her domains. According to *Fortune* and *CNNMoney*, Taylor Swift has already claimed URLs like TaylorSwift.porn before anyone else can. Being strategic about your domain ownership also applies to you, no matter where you are in your career.

MARCO...POLO?

How easy are you to contact? Let's face it: people have a short attention span. It has been said that we have a shorter attention span than a goldfish. If 57 percent of a purchase process is complete before a prospective client contacts you, but that potential client can't find an easy way to contact you, you may have blown a potential sale or a connection.

You need to make sure that your contact information is accessible. If you have a website, ideally your contact information should be at the top or bottom of the homepage to make it very easy to find. It can't be buried somewhere in the content.

Your contact information also needs to be listed clearly on your LinkedIn profile. This can be done in the contact section as well as the heading and in the summary section. It's easy to locate on your personal Facebook page's "About Me" section and on similar sections on your business's Facebook page, if you have one. If you use Twitter, then include contact information in your background image. Twitter gives you the option to upload a customized background image, which you can create yourself or hire someone to create for you.

You need to make your contact information easy to find because otherwise those potential clients or connections might find themselves frustrated and saying, "I don't have time to look for this," and go away. Once again, it's a missed opportunity to connect.

On occasion, I've had people push back and say, "But I don't want my contact information everywhere on the internet." If you're in business, you *should* have your contact information on the internet. You can do a couple of things, though, if having your personal contact information available online is a concern. If you don't feel comfortable publicizing your personal cell phone, then get a Google phone number by setting up a Google Voice account. The phone number is free, and you can forward calls to your home, cell, or business phone number. That way, people don't have direct access to your personal phone number. You might have a company email you can use instead of your personal email. You can also create a Gmail account that links to Google+ page so that people can see what city and state you're based in. You don't have to publicize your actual street address.

Regardless of what contact information you choose to use, make sure that your name, phone number, and email address are easily accessible in multiple places online. Not everyone uses every social media platform, so this will make it easier for others to find you and connect with you.

#CONNECTINGHACK

Vcita is a tool that allows site visitors to contact and even schedule appointments with you through a pop-up box on the homepage of your website.

SOCIAL CAPITAL

Now, let's talk about social media platforms. I know at this point you're probably thinking, "Wait a minute. Aren't we supposed to be talking about networking or connecting or whatever that is?" Well, yes.

But your best connections can happen in the most unusual places, both online and offline. If you think those connections are only going to happen at a networking event, you've already lost opportunities right there.

Talking about social media platforms in this book is essential because they give you the ability to create social capital. What's social capital? It's defined as the collective value of your online contacts. Your online relationships are a form of currency when it comes to connecting. And it isn't necessarily quantity of followers, friends, and connections but quality that's key.

Social media has changed the game with relationships because it gives you access to people you otherwise wouldn't have easy access to. You increase your social capital when you invest in your relationships by being as valuable as you possibly can in your networks. Your social capital is a measure of the degree of influence you have through your networks. The quality and quantity of your connections combined determine your online net worth and speaks to the influence of your brand.

What are you looking to accomplish? Take a moment to assess your business, your clients, and future clients. This will help you determine the best platforms to claim your space online. You have plenty of options, including LinkedIn, Facebook, Twitter, Google+, Pinterest, and YouTube. New platforms are being launched regularly, so it's impossible to keep up with the ones that come and go. To simplify things, we'll focus on the "'big six."

So what are the differences among them? LinkedIn is business-focused. Facebook and Google+ are a mixture of business-to-consumer and friend-to-friend. Twitter is a combination of the two. YouTube is the second-largest search engine behind Google and can be a powerful platform if video is your medium of choice. Pinterest was orignially seen as a personal platform but is quickly picking up steam in the business space.

No matter the platform, make sure that your online presence truly represents you. If your brand is mistmatched and inconsistent, people will be less likely to trust you and what you post.

Keep in mind that no social media platform will magically increase your visibility and social capital unless you understand how the platform works, what its users like, what they don't like, and what they want to see from you or your business.

I can't tell you how often I talk to people who say something like, "Oh yeah, I've set up a profiles on several sites, but I don't do anything with them." Once again, those are missed opportunities, because not taking the time to keep profiles active means you're not there to nurture potential connections.

If you're at the beginning stages of your business, consider which platforms you plan to use now and in the future. Check to see if they are available under your name or your business's name. Grab the platforms that are key to your connecting strategy. That doesn't mean you have to post content on all of them immediately. Just consider holding onto your social space.

I've also seen profiles that are out of date because their creators have changed positions, companies and even businesses (sometimes even as long as a year or more ago!). I may know your information is out of date, but you can't assume everyone knows. If I have an introduction I'd like to make, then inaccurate information is going to influence whether and how I make that introduction. If your contact information is too hard to find, I may just give up.

PHOTO SHOPPING

Have you heard that it takes seven seconds to make a first impression? Actually, one tenth of a second is much more accurate. A series of experiments by Princeton psychologists Janine Willis and Alexander Torodov revealed that it took just a tenth of a second to form an impression of strangers from their faces, and longer exposure doesn't significantly alter those impressions. (In case you missed it, the article, "First Impressions" was presented in the July 2006 issue of *Psychological Science.*) The goal of the research was to study judgments from facial appearance, focusing on different personal traits: attractiveness, likability, competence, trustworthiness, and aggressiveness. It didn't matter if the groups of participants had longer exposure times to the same photographs; once a judgment was made, it was unlikely to change.

It doesn't matter if you're preparing for a job interview or posting your photo on a social media platform like LinkedIn: you need to get your photo act together because people will judge you on your photo in the a blink of an eye (pun intended).

People connect to images 60,0000 times faster than text. Although the stakes may be high, you should still have the best photo possible of you on all of your online profiles and website rather than no photo at all. A pet peeve (and you'll see that I have several) is a social profile with no photo or a random icon in place of a photo. What's worse are the mug shots, party pics, or porn-star looks in photos on a business platform. You don't have to spend a small fortune to get a professional headshot done. You can accomplish your goal with your phone. Just make sure that your background isn't cluttered, because this will distract from your image, and that your clothing is appropriate. Now that I've mentioned it, you'll start to notice the good, the bad, and the really bad social profile photos of people you are connected with.

Your photo should be representative of the platforms that you are on. If you are your business, then a consistent profile photo across all platforms and websites may be the best route. If you're working for a company, then your bio on the company website and your Facebook profile don't need to be the same. In fact, it may look out-of-place to have a business image on a more casual site. The users on Twitter span such a wide variety of people and businesses that you have some choices here. The platform provides space for a customized background image along with a profile photo. If you're using Twitter as a business platform, then the photo should be consistent with your business brand. If you only use this for a personal site, then use what puts you in the best light. Don't use the default egg icon! Whatever photo and background image you use on Twitter, make it consistent with your brand.

Like the profile itself, your photo should be up-to-date. It's common to hear of stories about a photo posted on a dating site that in no way resembles the person who shows up for a first date. The same thing happens in business. And women, if you make a change in hair style—whether you wear your hair up or down, cut it shorter than it has been, or change the color—make sure that you have a current photo that matches your new style.

VANITY IS GOOD

If you're on a social site and you have the opportunity to get a vanity URL, you should take advantage of it. A vanity URL is a web address for the social media platform that includes your name or your business's name. A vanity URL is ideal if you're including it as part of your email signature—which we'll talk about shortly—or an online post or other communication.

For example, on LinkedIn, the default profile URL looks like this:

www.LinkedIn.com/profile/view?id=3100000&authType=name&authToken=1WaI&trk=mirror-profile-memberlist-name

A vanity URL can be customized. Mine is:

www.LinkedIn.com/in/JoyceLayman

If you do a Google search for my name, one of my top results is my LinkedIn profile via my LinkedIn vanity URL. It distinguishes me from everybody else and takes you right to my profile. Vanity URL's are also available on Facebook, Twitter, YouTube, Pinterest, Vimeo, Instagram, and more. If you're not familiar with how to make a vanity URL on the platforms you use, do a quick search for "creating a vanity URL" in the help section on each platform you're using.

Now, if you're a late adapter, the vanity URL of your name may already be gone. This is where you need to do a Google search of yourself to see who already has your name and what they are posting. Consider another version of your name if it's gone. If it isn't, *grab it right now* to make sure that you've got your social space claimed.

LINKEDIN AND BEYOND

It doesn't matter if you're working for somebody, if you have your own company, if you're thinking about starting a company, or you're in a career transition: LinkedIn is absolutely critical. It is the twelfth most-visited website on the internet. It typically shows up in the top three positions in Google searches if you make your profile and photo visible to everyone by adjusting your settings, complete your profile and update it regularly, post content, and send invitations to business colleagues or friends regularly.

Too often, the perception is that LinkedIn is only for an active job search. Not true! It's fantastic for business development to find potential clients, opening up the door for referral relationships, becoming a thought leader, and developing a following, or even just enhancing your personal brand. Maximizing your LinkedIn profile is the first step in how you do all of that.

Start with your headline. Your headline on a LinkedIn profile is vital for search functions. If you only list "CEO" as your job title or you only list "sales" but aren't specific to the industry, then you're missing out on valuable keyword opportunities because people are on LinkedIn to make connections, not just to find a job.

Your profile should be well-written to highlight the work you do and your expertise as well as to target your ideal clients and connections. Speaking in industry jargon doesn't cut it. And neither does looking like you're looking for a job, unless you really are. That is, you shouldn't write your profile like a resume, even if you are looking for a job. And it's worth mentioning again: your contact information must be easy to find so that people can actually reach out to you. Be sure to turn off the "Notify your network" setting on the right side of your profile. Otherwise, everyone you're connected to there will be notified each time you make even the smallest update to your profile. You'll get congratulations on the new position when you were just changing your headline title.

And if you don't have a clue about what to say on your LinkedIn page, hire somebody to help you make that happen. I have a couple of go-to folks in Kansas City whom I refer all of my clients to for crafting

LinkedIn profiles. As much time as I've spent to develop my presence on LinkedIn, I still want somebody sharp with an outside perspective to make sure that I have got my best brand forward, so to speak. Hopefully, you've got someone who is close to you who can help, or you can hire a professional writer to craft your profile. If you're looking for insight on crafting a LinkedIn profile, or how to maximize social media platforms in general, be sure to check out *Social Media Examiner*, the world's largest online social media magazine.

Your photo is just as important on LinkedIn as your other social profiles, especially for anyone in a career transition. The study by Alexander Torodov, mentioned previously, states it takes one-tenth of a second to make an impression, and it's mostly tone and face that influences total likability. A well-done photo can help your likability factor and also helps others remember you. That's significant and the very reason why it's critical for you to have that updated business photo.

When you're thinking about using LinkedIn, especially in a career transition, keep in mind just how much it can do for you. George Blomgren of MRA - The Management Association says that employers "will judge you not just on your profile but your overall mastery especially for IT, sales, marketing, human resources, and recruiting jobs. We look for professional headshot, a powerful summary, at least several hundred connections [your social capital], a complete employment history including descriptions, and a good list of relevant groups."

If you're one of those people who set up a LinkedIn profile some time ago and you think it's just one of those things that you don't have to keep up, you're missing out on opportunities. So spend some time to get it updated. It's worth the effort.

ALWAYS HAVE A PLAN B!

Did you know you can lose all of your LinkedIn contacts in an instant? If, for example, you're working for a company and all you have is that company email on your profile when you leave the company or when you get locked out of that email, you've just lost your entire base of relationships on LinkedIn. That means a lot of effort wasted, all because you didn't add a second email address.

Having two emails associated with you account provides an extra layer for securing your connections. The LinkedIn Help Center provides the following reasons that you should add a second email to make sure you never get accidentally locked out of your account:

- Most people add a work and a personal email. This provides an important backup in case you lose access to your primary email address (for example, if you change jobs and lose access to work email).

- If you only have one email address listed on your LinkedIn account and you lose access to it, we won't be able to send you a reset link if you forget your password. That means you won't be able to sign in to your LinkedIn account.

- It's important to add all email addresses that someone might use to connect with you on LinkedIn. If someone sends an invitation to an email address you haven't listed, you could get an error message or accidentally create a second account when you try to accept.

THE OTHER FINAL FOUR

Details make a difference. I'm surprised at how often folks miss the connecting basics: email address, email signature, business cards, and voicemail.

Did you know that the right email address can add value to your brand? Research by GoDaddy show that customers are nine times more likely to choose a business that uses a professional email address. This is critical. Even if you are an entrepreneur working at home or say, you've been a stay-at-home mom and you're looking into starting your own business and you've decided to go in direct sales, get an email that looks professional.

If you've already purchased a domain name for your business's website but are still using a Gmail account for your business email, you should look into changing your email address so that it matches your domain name. This is another low or no-cost adjustment you can make so that your website is consistent with your email address. And it certainly is those little details that some people would not notice but folks like me will always notice. There needs to be consistency, just like with online profiles. There needs to be consistency with messaging the brand of you.

For example, if your email address was zoe9399@emaildomain.com but your company's website is www.xyzconsultingcompany.com, your email address should at least be xyzconsultingcompany@emaildomain.com or, ideally, zoe@xyzconsulting.com.

If you're in a career transition, an email address is just as important for a professional appearance. If you haven't already, consider setting up a Gmail account with YourName@gmail.com (or Your.Name@gmail.com or Firstname.Middleinitial.Lastname@gmail.com).

There are other email providers you can use. Gmail is just one example. What's important is that you not use some wonky email handle instead of your name. Sending an email from imachocolatelover@emaildomain.com isn't going to put you in the best light.

When it comes to the content of your emails, remember that poor grammar in an email leaves a bad impression. I realize that we're so used to texting and doing things in short verse that some people have forgotten the art of communication. Once again, this could be the first time somebody has had an interaction with you, so make sure that that email comes across clearly and correctly.

There are some corporate services that will check over emails for grammatical correctness (Grammarly is one). You can also find copyediting and copywriting freelancers easily through the Editorial Freelancers Association and UpWork, and chances are that someone in your network already has an arrangement or connection with a freelancer whom they'd be happy to recommend to you. That being said, I happen to know several freelancers who are fantastic to work with!

It's possible to set up an arrangement with the freelancer for quick email corrections for important emails or to develop boilerplate emails that can be easily adapted for future use. Another tip is to ask someone else to read drafts of emails aloud before they go out. Keep a usage—not just a regular—dictionary close by for questions about when to use certain phrases or words.

When people are introduced to you via email, it may be the first time that someone has had an interaction with you, so including your email signature in the email is vitally important. In your email signature, you should have a link to the social sites that you're on and to your websites. This is part of what it means to make it easy for people to find out more information about you, to click just once to get directly to your website and social profiles so they can find what they're looking for to help them make the decision to choose you.

If you're saying, "What do I do for an email signature?", a good way to start is to do a Google search for example email signatures. But if you're challenged when it comes to technology and need somebody to create and insert a logo into your email, then go to Fiverr. Search email signatures there and you'll find numerous folks who will create a custom email signature for $5. It's worth it.

#CONNECTINGHACK

My favorite #connectinghack of all hacks is Crystal. Crystal is an email tool that you download to help you to communicate empathetically with another person. It's almost scary what Crystal can do with internet research to find out about the other person's personality and their style based on their social profiles. Crystal gives you a profile assessment and tips for how to communicate more effectively with that person. Communicating how the other person wants to be communicated with is a connecting advantage.

DON'T FORGET THE CARDS

Your business card is critical when you're looking at the "final four." Your card can be a way of making an initial impression when you're at an event and you meet somebody who says, "Hey, I'd like a business card." What does your card say about you? Is it easy to read? Do you have all sorts of jargon that might make sense to someone in your industry but leaves the rest of us perplexed? It may be better to be simple than have too much.

But like with your email address, make sure that your business card presents you in the best light, especially if you're in a career transition. There are lots of websites—Vistaprint and Moo, just to name two—where you can get professional business cards for a very small investment. It's worth it because nothing looks more unprofessional than writing your information on a piece of paper. You can get away with that on rare occasion. It's not the ideal way to make a connection, but it's better than not getting a chance to follow up on a great conversation. On occasion, I have attended an event and had so many people asking me for cards that I gave away all that I had with me. In that case, if people ask me for a card, I will take their cards and make sure that I get in contact with them immediately.

And remember to carry business cards with you at all times if possible. If you're at the gym, for example, and pockets aren't an option, know what your backup plan is. If you forget your cards or—for ladies—forgot to make sure you had cards when you changed your purse, a suggestion is to put a stack in the glove compartment of your car or to carry extras in your computer bag.

I'M NOT SURE I HAVE THE RIGHT NUMBER...

The final connecting basic is your voicemail message. If you give out your cell phone for business and potential clients call you but there is no voicemail greeting or you have the canned "You've reached 000-000-0000" message, you risk confusing that potential client. The impersonal message might also leave them with a less-than-stellar impression of you. This is also a risk you take if your voicemail is full and no one can leave a message. If they get the generic message that tells them you can't be reached this way, they may not call back.

Your voicemail greeting should be short, to the point and provide clear direction for the caller. As a keynote speaker, I can tell you that if you stand and smile you have a different emphasis in your voice and better projection. Your posture also affects your tone, and it translates through to the other end of the phone.

It's also important to make sure you're keeping your greeting up-to-date. I recently switched phone carriers and realized two days after the switch that I hadn't set up the new greeting because I was so used to having the other greeting. Consider changing your greeting once every three months or every six months. You don't have to create the same message every time. Ask callers to let you know in their message when a good time to call them back would be. It can help keep you out of phone tag. Regardless of what you choose to say in your greeting, get it set up if you haven't already. It's free. It only takes a few minutes.

VANILLA SEAS

If you want to be successful, creating a personal brand isn't just an option. It's a necessity. A well-thought-out and well-executed personal brand can help you stand out in a sea of vanilla. Whether your goal is to get a promotion, land a client, or make a strategic connection, creating a compelling and consistent brand is critcal to your connecting advantage.

Start by being memorable online. If you look like everyone else or no one at all, you'll soon be an afterthought. Before you ever go to a networking event or any event for that matter, make sure that your personal brand is ready to represent you, because your best connections can happen anywhere and anytime. In fact, your best connections may have already Googled you, and you want to be ready to connect.

ACTION

Now that you're to the end of chapter one it's time to take action on the top three things you feel are most important to your connecting advantage strategy right now. To stay focused and not be overwhelmed, just focus on the top three for now.

As mentioned in the introduction, the steps are delineated by the amount of time it will take you to accomplish them: up to 15 minutes or up to an hour and more. You know your ability far better than anyone else, so if you're unfamiliar with one of the things on your list, estimate the time as best you can.

Fast Start

One-Hour Win

Snail It

CHAPTER 2

VALUE PROPS, LOGLINES, AND VIRTUAL STALKING

WHAT'S YOUR WOW FACTOR?

The term "value proposition" is usually aligned with the marketing and sales of a product or service. It's the compelling reason someone would want to do business with you. In the context of this book, I'm expanding the definition to include the value you bring to others when they choose to connect with you. The result could be a new client, strategic alliance, resource, friendship, running buddy, and more. Remember, we're talking about connecting, not just networking.

Just like your brand, your value proposition needs to be clearly understood. Too often, I find that people tend to stick with the typical language used within their industry. They follow traditional marketing tactics of sharing what they do best instead of considering the challenges and frustrations that the other person (as in, a potential client) is experiencing.

As mentioned in the introduction, I came across a number of experts while doing research for the book, one of them being Dorie Clark. Dorie is a marketing strategy consultant and is considered a branding expert by the Associated Press, *Fortune*, and *Inc. Magazine* and is on the "#Nifty50 list of top women on twitter." Her diverse background made her passionate about helping others make their mark in the world. Her book *Reinventing You* was published in 2013, and *Stand Out* is her most recent book. Budding thought leaders (which we'll cover in chapter nine) need to read *Stand Out* cover to cover.

For those who need help defining their uniqueness and value, start by answering the following five questions Dorie poses in "Your Stand Out Self-Assessment: 139 Questions to Help You Find Your Breakthrough Idea and Build a Following Around It," which you can find on her website. **www.dorieclark.com**

Question 1: What are others in your field overlooking?

Question 8: What are three trends shaping your industry? Are they short-term or fundamental? How would you describe them to an outsider unfamiliar with your field?

Question 12: What innovations or new developments do you know about that most others do not?

Question 16: What experiences have you had that others in your field most likely have not? How does that difference shape your view of the industry?

Question 20: Is there a way you can differentiate yourself from others in your profession?

Answering these questions will get you thinking differently about your personal brand, your business, and, in turn, the value you provide to the connections you want to make. Your answers will also help you with your message and with crafting your logline and 30-second commercial, which we'll dive into shortly. These are critical for differentiating yourself in a sea of vanilla.

If you really want to take a deep dive, don't stop with just these five questions. Go to Dorie's website and download the entire assessment. If you just had a small heart attack over the thought of doing even more work, it's going to be ok. You made it to the second chapter of *Your Connecting Advantage*, and that alone speaks volumes!

FOCUS ON THE TALK, NOT THE PITCH

Now that you're well armed with new information, it's time to talk about how to put it into action. When you initially meet someone, the goal is simply to connect. Pique their curiosity and learn about them, too. This isn't the same as selling because you never know where you'll be when you make a connection. It could even start online. If you get stumped after the "Hi, how are you" stage, it could be because you're too focused on an outcome rather than an initial conversation and seeing where it might lead. But if you don't know the best way to introduce yourself and your business or to explain why you're looking to connect, then how can you expect anyone else to understand?

It's not just what you say but the approach as well. Have you experienced the three-foot rule? If you haven't heard of it, the three-foot rule means that if you're within three feet of someone who's purely focused on making a sale, you've become a prime target for that person. It can be an uncomfortable position to be in, especially if this is the first time that you've met this person. I hear feedback that networking events are all about sales. Folks assume that people who approach them at events are only interested in how quickly they can close a deal instead of simply trying to have a conversation. Be open to the possibility of a great connection. And, whatever you do, don't be the three-foot rule guy! When you start with the intent of adding value, meaningful relationships can happen as a result. No matter whom you're meeting or where, don't wing this. You may have one chance to get it right!

You've probably heard of the idea of being ready with a 30-second commercial or elevator speech to introduce yourself or your business. You're going to want one for yourself, but we're not going to start there. The first step in developing a strategy for communicating your value is something you're probably less familiar with: loglines.

LOGLINES AND INTROS

Can you sum up your value in one sentence that's easy to understand, engages the person you're talking to, and answers the question, "What do you do?" When pitching a movie, the term is called the "logline." It's a one- or two-sentence summary of a script. It explains what the movie is about and helps you decide if you're interested in seeing it. The following movie loglines may sound familiar (credit: IMDB):

- A classic fairy tale, with swordplay, giants, an evil prince, a beautiful princess, and yes, some kissing (as read by a kindly grandfather).

- A journey of self-discovery by a brilliant mathematician once he was diagnosed with schizophrenia. He eventually triumphs over tragedy and receives the Nobel prize.

- When a Roman general is betrayed and his family murdered by a corrupt prince, he comes to Rome as a gladiator to seek his revenge.

If an Academy-Award-nominated film can be boiled down a simple sentence, then you can boil down your answer to a question, "What do you do?" into a logline, too.

In connecting terms, your logline is the sentence that will pique someone's curiosity to have a conversation. This isn't about telling someone how you do what you do, giving technical information, or pulling a Jerry McGuire. You may not get them at "Hello" if you share too much. Microsoft recently studied human attention spans and found out that people who use smartphones regularly have an attention span of eight seconds. Goldfish have an attention span of nine seconds. That's why it's imperative to be brief.

Your logline isn't a one-size-fits-all statement, and it's not to be confused with a 30-second commercial. It will change depending on your audience. What you say at a formal networking event could be different from what you say when you're sitting at a soccer game or making a connection on an airplane. The point is to be prepared, because your best connections can happen anyplace, anytime.

We've already covered the fact that that it takes one tenth of a second to make an impression and that it's much harder to get people to shift their perceptions once they're formed. Making something up on the spot or sounding too contrived doesn't leave the best impression. This doesn't mean waiting until an opportunity happens. Take time to craft what you will say and tweak it once you've had the opportunity to "test" it. You can always share it with a few friends or business associates who know you to get their reactions.

THAT "ONE THING"

In your logline, talk about one idea, not many, and be as specific as possible. You can't be all things to all people.

Make your logline relatable. That means taking the industry-speak out of your vocabulary and keeping it in layman's terms. If you're crafting a logline in hopes of connecting with potential clients, focus on the problems they have that you can help solve, not the benefits that you offer. You also want to be aware of what makes you unique from your competition. Look back to your answers to the five questions from "Your Stand Out Self-Assessment" for additional insight.

If this is a one-on-one conversation, then knowing a little bit about the other person is helpful to guide you, which means you need to ask questions first. If you don't have that opportunity, use the default logline that you've already crafted that best describes what you do in way that provides clarity for the person you are talking with.

When asked what I do, I used to say, "I do keynote speaking." The response typically was, "Oh, you're a motivational speaker." People already had formed their perception of what I do. Keynote speaking is just one of the services I provide, and unless they were looking to hire a speaker, their eight-second attention span shifted to something else, if they didn't see another reason to connect.

My loglines now include:

- "I connect people." (Super short but effective.)
- "I'm a professional wing-woman."
- "I show people how to stop wasting time at networking events."
- "I teach people how to create opportunities from the relationships they already have."

Do you have currently have a logline you use? If not, ponder these questions to get the creative juices flowing to make your own logline:

- Who is the person or audience you're looking to connect with?
- What's their biggest frustration?
- What problem do you solve for your clients?
- What are you passionate about?
- What are you really good at?
- What resources do you need?

After you get your ideas together, you can do the following mini-exercises to spark some ideas:

- Do a short brainstorming session and write down everything that comes to mind when someone asks, "What do you do?" Think about why someone would hire you and what problems you solve.

- The next step is to cut out jargon or clichés. For example: "We help you do more with less, take your business to the next level, and shift paradigms," etc.

- Now write out one-sentence loglines. You'll have several depending on whether you're talking to a potential client or looking for a resource or strategic partner.

If you have several loglines that you really like, then you could even set up a logline bracket to determine which one is the first winner. I say "first" because ultimately you'll want to have several winning loglines.

A well-received logline can open the door to continuing a conversation, but only if you pause long enough to give the other person time to ponder what you just said. When they ask, "What do you mean by that?", you've been given the permission share a little more information.

STUCK IN AN ELEVATOR

The next step is to craft a 30-second commercial, also known as an elevator speech or elevator pitch. Just like life, 30-second commercials evolve, so even if you already have one crafted, this section may spark a new spin on it. According to the Graziadio School of Business and Management at Pepperdine University, elevator speeches evolved during the early days of the Internet explosion when web development companies were courting venture capital. Finance firms were swamped with applications for money, and the companies that won the cash were often those with a simple pitch. The best were those who could explain a business proposition to the occupants of an elevator in the time it took them to ride to their floor. In other words, an elevator speech that worked would describe and sell an idea in 30 seconds or less.

You have approximately 30 seconds to a minute, max, to deliver your "commercial." This sounds like a very short amount of time, but when crafted in the right way, it can open doors. Too often, people equate a 30 second commercial with sales. But your commercial could also be about a resource or information that you need. So don't think that when you're crafting a 30 second commercial, it's all about pitching your business, product, or service.

Please don't pitch. This is about connecting, engaging by sharing very short story (a few sentences long). If you come across as a salesperson or go into the three-foot rule mode, people will tune you out. Remember the goldfish. The point, once again, is simply to engage and connect. Stay "them-focused" instead of "you-focused."

Your 30-second commercial will be slightly different depending on whether you're standing in front of a group to introduce yourself or speaking with someone one-on-one. There are many people who work in the same industry with the same qualifications that you have. It seems like people in insurance, banking, financial services, etc., tend to travel in packs at the same networking events. In a group of 30-40 people, you could easily have three to five duplicated services or qualifications.

BLAH, BLAH, BLAH

A typical 30-second commercial tends to start off with, "Hi, my name is Sam. I work for XYZ company and we do blah blah blah." If your 30-second commercial starts that way, you've lost just about everyone.

When you have 40 people in a room, you'll notice that most start their 30-second commercials this way because that's what is expected and, unfortunately, encouraged. Did you know your brain processes over 400 billion bits of information every second? Needless to say, there's a lot fighting for your attention, like the cell phone in your hand or the side conversation you've got going on. (Yes, I just called you out!)

The best way to get someone's attention is to start with a pattern and then break the pattern. For example, you can begin your 30-second commercial by asking a question with an emotional appeal that your audience can relate to. This keeps you from being lost in a vanilla sea and sounding like everyone else.

One of my opening lines is, "Have you ever left a networking event feeling like you just wasted an hour of your time?" It's easy to see by the looks on people's faces and the occasional nod that they've had that experience. Now, I've got their attention.

People remember stories, so opening a 30-second commercial with a story that speaks to the problems you solve and then to the services you can offer. This isn't about telling them everything you do in that moment otherwise they could run for the hills. Think about an example of how you helped someone in a situation that's similar to one that would speak to your audience. Tell your audience about that situation in a super-short story that then prompts them to action. If you need a quick resource for crafting an opening, you can rely on the story technique.

Another great opening is to share a statistic or some other factual information. If you choose to go this route, be sure to have additional facts that you could share later when the actual conversations start. Leave the industry-speak at the office. And a reminder: no clichés!

HO HUM TO HOT DAMN

One of my coaching clients, Martha Childers, needed help crafting her 30-second commercial after making a career transition. Martha has a fascinating background. She was a librarian and lived in numerous places around the world To be successful in her position, she learned to speak three languages in addition to English. Martha made the leap from working for someone else to working for herself, and networking was part of her business development strategy. She was soft-spoken and uncomfortable standing up in front a group to give her 30-second commercial. The first time I heard it, it went something like this: "Hello. My name is Martha, and I'm a therapist and do couples counseling. My office is located on the Plaza." It was vague and didn't really grab her audience emotionally.

Time to get out of vanilla. We started her commercial with something unique: the first sentence was spoken in Japanese. Then she said, "In case you didn't understand me, I just said that my husband doesn't listen to me. My name is Martha Childers, and I'm a therapist. I speak three foreign languages, and one of my specialties is multicultural relationships. What I do is help couples to really hear each other so they can get to the heart of the matter. In turn, they get their relationships back on track and have the communication tools to keep it on track. If this sounds like something that speaks to your needs, maybe we should talk."

You should have seen people's heads whip around when she started speaking in Japanese. They were completely focused on what she was going to say next. If you paid attention to the words, she didn't start with her name. She also said, "One of my specialties is…" That leads the listener to think there are many things she does well. Too often, people try to wrap everything up they do into one 30-second commercial, which goes by so quickly that listeners can't pick up on all the information that speaks to them. It's imperative that you get to one specialty or one area of expertise and focus just on that.

Martha was a little uncomfortable delivering her 30-second commercial from memory, so I had her print it off and read it. It's better to read it than to get nervous and miss key points, because if speaking in public is one of your fears, then having to speak from memory is going to reinforce that fear in your mind and make it even harder. This is ideal for wallflowers and those you who are brand new to sharing your commercial at a networking event. Even though it may feel like you're giving a keynote, it's only 30 seconds.

Another tip: practice reading your 30-second commercial out loud before you get to an event where you have to deliver it. This will help you get warmed up, and it will sound closer to what you're actually going to say than it would if you only read it quietly to yourself. Just be aware that you can over-rehearse. Then if something happens that takes you off track or distracts you—you could get a laugh from the group, or someone's phone might ring—then you might have trouble getting back on track. Practice, but trust your natural conversation skills to guide you. Take note of how the group reacts to what you say. The whole point of being able to get feedback is doing it well and doing it in public.

YOUR 30 SECONDS

You may already have a 30-second commercial that's turning heads. Below are some tips for creating it or perfecting it. Refer back to what you wrote down for your logline and expand on it even further. When crafted correctly the listener should learn: your name, business, what type of problems you solve, and what makes you different from others in your line of work.

Use the following as your guide:

- Open with an attention getting statement or question.

- Add one specialty or one problem you solve. Include the benefit to them and a question/s that motivates them to connect with you.

- Introduce yourself and your business.

Go for short sentences that use strong verbs and carefully-chosen adjectives or emotion words to shape your story. Reorder sentences if needed and then connect them to each other, so that they tell the story of what you do for your clients. Be sure to introduce yourself and your business in the middle or at the end, never at the beginning.

I'm always listening for stellar 30-second commercials, and Greta Perel has one of the best. Considering she's a professional writer, it's to be expected. She's given me permission to share her loglines and 30-second commercial with you:

One-on-one conversation: "I show people how to persuade, motivate, and wow their audiences."

Longline introduction in front of a group: "If you want to persuade, motivate, and WOW! your audience, talk to me."

30-second commercial: "Have you ever had to give a presentation before? How did you feel? Stressed? Terrified? Why? Maybe you didn't know where to start? Maybe you didn't know what to say? If you want to persuade, motivate, and WOW! your audience every time, talk to me. I'm a speechwriter and a writer, and my name is Greta Perel."

Don't wait till you're at an event to craft your logline or 30-second commercial. Getting it right takes a little time. It's worth it!

VIRTUAL STALKING

Another part of defining your value proposition involves researching the person you want to connect with. If you have a one-on-one meeting scheduled or are going to a particular event and you know someone whom you've been hoping to meet will be there, then do a little research first. This isn't stalking; it's research. If only I had coined the term! The point is to do your homework.

When you're looking to create great relationships, start by finding common ground. Reaching out to someone on LinkedIn and saying, "I see we're connected through Joe, and your business could really use my service. Can we talk?" is a poor approach. The same hold true for reaching out to someone and asking them to make an introduction on your behalf when they hardly know you. Because you haven't taken time to develop a relationship with either person, you're taking a shot in the dark. You have no clear sense of the value you can offer that person you're attempting to do business with or to the person you're asking to make a connection for you. You may be able to find common ground with that person by doing some research first. Consider mutual connections with friends and business associates whom you value. What do they know about this person and the person's business?

That individual may look like a potential client or strategic resource, but that doesn't necessarily mean he or she would be a good connection. It's better to find out a little about how someone operates in business and life first. Once you have a few details about that person's business, then find out if you and the person you're researching have any special interests in common like hobbies, serving on non-profit boards, music, etc. Now, you most likely won't have mutual interests with everyone you want to meet. But when you can find those commonalities, that's great for developing a stronger connection. Look for ways to start meaningful conversations.

Do a quick Google search of the names of new connections to see what comes up first. Depending on the effort they put into their brands, you could find numerous starting points. On occasion, I run across people who have done very little on social media, and the organizations they are with don't have staff listed on their websites. Researching those folks takes more effort.

I've also met one person who paid to have every scrap of information about themselves taken off the internet. Doing that is a big investment. They had sold their interest in a company and is preferring to stay off the Google radar so to speak.

With me, my website comes up first and then my LinkedIn profile. There's lots of information about me that's easily accessible. The key is to be thorough when researching someone. Read their headlines and summary section and then keep scrolling.

If you took time to read through my LinkedIn profile, you would see at first glance that I speak four languages. But in actuality, what I have written is: "English as native or bilingual proficiency. Body: professional working proficiency. Silence: full professional proficiency. Gibberish: professional working proficiency." For people who know me, they know that this is my sense of humor. And for the people who don't know me, it makes them pause. I've had two people comment on the language portion of my profile because they actually caught it. That tells me that they're paying attention and being thorough in their research.

If the company website shows up first for the people you are researching, start there. Otherwise, you can start by reviewing information on the LinkedIn profiles (if they have profiles filled out), but don't stop there. Look at the other top results to see which social media platforms you are both on. Are they on Facebook? If so, look to see if you have any mutual connections. Their privacy settings will determine if you can see their posts, photos and other information. If you are both on Twitter, then you can see what they're posting as long as their settings are public. (Note: if you're on Twitter and using the platform for business, be sure your posts are public and not protected. Otherwise, you have to approve everyone who sees them.) Depending on their business and other interests, they may also have Pinterest,

Instagram, and YouTube accounts. Don't forget to check out their websites and blogs, too.

IT'S NOT STALKING, IT'S RESEARCH

As an example, let me tell you about how I approached the CEO of a technology company in Kansas City whom I wanted to connect with. I had read an article about him in the *Kansas City Business Magazine*. I was impressed with what he said about corporate culture. The article also shared that he flew attack helicopters in the Persian Gulf. He just seemed like a super cool dude.

Because I wanted to know more about he and his company, my first step was to go to the company website, I did a quick review of the "About" page and then the "Leadership Team" page to see if I recognized any of his key leaders. It was on the website that I found the links to his personal blog, so I skimmed a couple of blog posts. The links to his social sites were also there, so I clicked on the one to his LinkedIn profile, but I didn't immediately reach out to connect with him because he didn't know who I was. Next, I went to Twitter, and that's when I discovered that he is very active on Twitter. As the CEO of a technology company, it made perfect sense. I followed him and then retweeted some of his posts. The interesting thing was that later that day, he reached out to me with a request to connect on LinkedIn. He was the one who suggested we meet for a cup of coffee because he just likes getting to know other people. The coffee lasted an hour and a half. Our conversation spanned corporate culture, mutual connections, and his interests in veterans. That was just the beginning. In case you're wondering, the research I did to connect with him took less than 15 minutes.

I discovered that if I sent him an email, I typically waited up to 24 hours to get a response. Tweeting or sending him a direct message got a quicker response. You may need to get out of your technology/social media comfort zone to connect with people where they are, especially when it comes to clients and key connections.

When it comes to social media—if you haven't noticed—people often post personal as well as business information. Maybe their kids won a baseball game, or maybe there was a new addition to the family, or maybe they won an award in business. Would any of those things be about hobbies that you have in common? If not, maybe there's at least an opportunity to connect by offering congratulations.

#CONNECTINGHACK

There are several hacks that can help you to simplify your research process and save time. The first is a customer relationship management (CRM) tool called Nimble. It combines a CRM with the power of social media. Nimble helps you keep notes while you're doing research on someone and keeps all of that information together and easily accessible. Once you set up a profile for a connection, Nimble will update your notes in real time with the latest posts and updates that person is sharing on social media. There are other CRM's that I will mention throughout, but when your focus is the social media side, this a great option.

If you already have a CRM, then consider Rapportive. It's a great connecting hack that ties into your Gmail account. When you click on a contact to craft an email, Rapportive automatically pulls up that person's social media platforms and updates. So if you just want a quick glance of what that connection posted recently, it's right there.

Value props, loglines, 30-second commercials, virtual stalking (the good kind): these are all things that are going to help you stand out in the crowd because they can help you show that you value relationships. A little prep time can turn an expected or unexpected meeting into a world of opportunities.

ACTION

Now that you're to the end of chapter two, it's time to take action on the top three things you feel are most important to your connecting advantage strategy right now.

Fast Start

One-Hour Win

Snail It

CHAPTER 3

HEAD GAMES, MINDSETS, AND THAT NEW GUY

The term *networking* has a tendency to make people feel uncomfortable. It conjures up an image of an event with a large group of people, the majority of whom you don't know, who're all having awkward conversations about what they do for a living and handing out as many cards as possible in the hopes that they will turn someone there into a client or help you in some other way.

For those who thrive on situations like this, you've found networking nirvana. For the rest, it's a mini-version of hell on a weeknight.

Tiziana Casciaro—a professor of organizational behavior at the University of Toronto—and some of her colleagues surveyed more than 700 working adults and lawyers about how often they attend networking events and how they feel about networking. Their responses were probably similar to yours: they often felt "morally impure" and a desire "to literally cleanse themselves" after attending networking events, partly because they viewed networking as a time when they have to be self-serving and self-promoting, and they tended to be more demoralized about their work if they frequently attended networking events. But the study also showed a correlation between networking and promotions for senior-level partners in law firms. Casciaro and her colleagues found that senior partners had a more positive attitude toward networking and were more likely to have a higher level of engagement at business networking events. They felt more authentic about the networking events they participated in.

And here you thought it was just you. It's not the situation but your mindset that determines how events will unfold and if you'll be creating authentic connections (for business or personal interests) or just wasting another hour of time. As a recovering wallflower who hesitated to attend an event and wouldn't start a conversation to save my life, I can relate.

HEAD GAMES

One of the questions I'm asked on a regular basis is, "How did you get to the point where you felt comfortable walking into a room full of strangers and striking up a conversation?" Had you met me back in 2005, you would have seen me as more of the wallflower type. I was in a sales position and felt perfectly comfortable in one-on-one meetings. But put me in a Chamber happy hour, and I was the wallflower standing next to the food table.

One of the things that helped me make the shift was a desire to learn how to network (that's what I called it back then). After that, the next step was to get out of my own way. But the problem was that I didn't know what that was.

I shared the story in my book *Just Another Leap* about meeting Denise Mills—the woman who changed my life—and the series of events that unfolded because of that connection. They say that when the student is ready, the teacher will appear, and that was certainly the case for me. In 2005, I was at a networking event where I was listening to a woman give a presentation. She was one of those people who lit up the room when she walked in. I remember looking at her as she was talking and thinking to myself, "I don't know what that is, but I want some of what she's got."

Back then, it was really outside my comfort zone to walk up and talk to somebody who had just been speaking. But this time, I went over and introduced myself to Denise. I asked, "Where do I get more information about what you were sharing with us?" She said, "Well, I'm speaking on the same topic tomorrow for another group."

The next day, I went to hear her speak on the very same topic. I was mesmerized, totally caught up in whatever it was that she had.

I talked to her again after her speech that next day and we scheduled a coffee meeting. It was at that meeting she suggested I go through a program that significantly influenced her life. Her invitation was an easy "Yes" for me, and those lightbulb moments—as I was learning the concepts in the program—were so numerous, it was like there were paparazzi in my head.

This program gave me the cognitive tools to understand finally how I had created my own limiting beliefs. I started becoming more aware of what I was thinking. I knew why I had become a wallflower. I also knew why I wasn't accomplishing everything that I wanted to in my business. In the past, I had worked with coaches and identified goals, but I kept pulling back and wouldn't take the steps to accomplish those goals. I wasn't working to my potential. After going through the program, my eyes were opened to new possibilities, and it was a huge turning point in my life.

I realized that making connections was the very thing that I needed to get me where I wanted to be in my business. I just wasn't sure of the steps to take to make those connections happen. I also had to shift out of the mindset that it was "all about me." Just as predicted in the study mentioned above, my mindset contributed to the awkwardness I felt at networking events.

Fortunately, at this time I discovered two books by Bob Burg that influenced my life in a big way: *Endless Referrals* and *The Go-Giver*. The first was what I call my "networking bible." It's got a step-by-step process, and I'm all about process. Bob mentions successful giving and receiving, which was a mental shift for me. *The Go-Giver*, written in conjunction with John David Mann, was written as a business parable. It spoke directly to five powerful laws: value, compensation, influence, authenticity, and receptivity. To borrow a cliché, it was a huge paradigm shift for me, and knowing that focusing on others would come back 10-fold made it easier to do things—like talking to strangers—that pushed me outside of my comfort zone.

This information, combined with my training in The Pacific Institute's processes, was the foundation for my business. TPI's processes weren't about the soft and fluffy stuff but about helping me to understand how my mind works at the conscious and subconscious levels. What I learned is that the greatest obstacle I was facing was the four inches between my ears.

Part of the mental processes I was learning about at the time involved intentionally doing things that would push me. These included big things—like tackling my fear of heights—and simple things—like switching toenail polish or driving a different way to get to a meeting. All of these things helped me to get comfortable with being uncomfortable. The more intentional I was, I realized that feeling uncomfortable was actually part of the process for growth.

I was intent on acquiring the skillset and tactics I need to use in order to build my network. The thing is, introverts and wallflowers have a tendency to hang out with the folks they already know instead of making new connections. This means that they miss a lot of opportunities. I'd already been stuck there, so my problem was that I went on networking-event overdrive with the intent of attending everything I could. I was going for quantity rather than quality. I had the steps but was doing it without a strategy.

MINDSETS

Many people will tell you how to network, but few of them talk about why it's so hard for some people. Think about the differences between introverts and extroverts. Extroverts are the folks who seem to be the life of the party. They can walk into a room full of strangers and do just fine. It's the introverts who have a problem reaching out to make a connection. There's a third category that you may not be familiar with: ambivert. These folks are people whose personalities have both extrovert and introvert features, but neither is dominant.

According to Adam Grant, an organizational psychologist at the University of Pennsylvania's Wharton School and author of *Give and Take*, more than half the population is ambiverted. "Ambiverts are like Goldilocks," Grant explains. "They offer neither too much nor too little."

The thing to be careful of is not defining what you're capable of when labeling your personality traits because everyone is equally capable of developing great relationships. The trick is figuring out what you're really good at, the best events for you to attend so you can shine, and getting the mental tools to help you get over hurdles that may be stopping you from creating those great relationships.

If the thought of attending an event with a lot of people sends you back to your desk, this could simply be situational introversion. As much as I enjoy getting out, there are certain locations that make me feel out of place and other places where I'm the life of the party.

One of the biggest hurdles can be comfort zones. In *Just Another Leap*, I defined comfort zones as behavioral spaces that help you minimize stress and risk. Comfort zones can be behavioral but they can also be physical spaces, like a networking event.

If you step outside of your comfort zone, you may find yourself stepping into or creating stories or beliefs that may or may not be true. Be careful not to get caught in the cycle of the stories and beliefs that aren't true. Take a step back and do a reality check. Ask yourself if the story or belief is true—*really* true—and if you're embellishing or telling yourself a story about yourself to avoid something you fear, create a new story instead.

When you're stretched to the edge of your comfort zone, your brain grows. It's not easy to do what's hard and uncomfortable. For me, I know that extraordinary connections have resulted because I stepped out of my comfort zone.

THIS, THAT, AND IN BETWEEN

Our beliefs about who we are shape how we see ourselves and what we can do. Even though I was already aware of this, reading business management and motivation expert Daniel Pink's book *To Sell Is Human,* provided new insight. In that book, Pink focuses on the art and science of selling. One of the tools I found helpful was an assessment he created, and it's available on his website. So, go to his website to take this quick assessment for yourself and determine whether you are an introvert, extrovert, or an ambivert.

www.danpink.com/assessment/

Even though I once believed that I was a wallflower, I had come to think of myself as an extrovert until I went through Pink's assessment.

Ambivert suits me to a tee. Whether delivering a keynote or facilitating a connecting event, I love being with groups of people. I discovered that to be at my best, I need to recharge by myself, preferably by cycling, doing yard work, or spending time in my loft. As long as I'm alone to recharge sometimes, life is good. That's what makes me an ambivert.

If you believe you're more introverted or have more wallflower tendencies, then push your comfort zone in increments. What I mean by this is that instead of starting by going into a big room full of strangers at a business event and trying to talk to everyone, try making a comment to someone while standing in line to get coffee. Offer that person a compliment. State the obvious about the day. See if you can make the people around you laugh.

The point of starting with small steps is to practice talking to strangers. As cliché as it sounds, your fear of starting up conversations might actually be a buried belief that you have because you were told at an early age, "Don't talk to strangers." Some of us truly took that to heart, and it shaped our beliefs about how to interact with others. Years later, it's still influencing our actions. Pay attention to the stories you tell yourself because they may or may not be true.

CONVERSATION COMFORT

Edith Wharton once said, "Ah good conversation, there's nothing like it, is there? The air of ideas is the only air worth breathing." When it comes to coping with the pressures of networking, sometimes no networking is really the best networking. If you're just one of those folks who gets completely frozen when you walk into a networking event, then practice having conversations in places outside of formal business events. Maybe it's at church, your kid's soccer game, standing in line at the grocery store, the gym, or someplace else. Again, the point is just to get comfortable as you go along.

Having a conversation with somebody when you're in your comfort zone—like during a casual morning jog or having coffee—tends to be more authentic and a lot more fun. And when you're connecting over mutual interests, your conversations can be more lasting.

If you're attending an actual business event, then one of the things that you can do to build confidence is to practice in your mind before you go. Think back to the last time you made a great connection. What did it feel like? How did you approach the person you wanted to talk to, or did that person approach you? What did you say to kick off the conversation? What did the other person say to keep everything flowing? Did you physically feel nervous or comfortable?

I know it sounds a little odd to mentally rehearse a conversation, but athletes use that technique to help their sports performance. They mentally simulate the perfect swing, lift, or kick. Musicians also do this sort of mental practice, practicing scales and hearing the music they're going to play before they start playing. They mentally simulate tones and rhythms so they know what they *want* to sound like before they even start playing.

Visualizing what you want to achieve and how you want to achieve it can help you step out of your comfort zones. So if talking to strangers a sticking point for you, try practicing in your mind first.

Another strategy you can use is to take a wingman or wing-woman with you. The whole point of making connections is to meet other people, not to spend all of your time with the people you already know. So if you go to a networking event with a wingman, then you need to have a plan for navigating your way around the event. One way to do this is to stay together and when you see someone whom you know but your wingman doesn't or vice versa, you can make introductions for each other. Another option is to divide and conquer, so to speak, by going off on your own and make a couple of connections. If you meet someone you feel would be a good connection for your fellow wingman, bring that person to introduce to your wingman. This accomplishes two things. First, it takes the pressure off you because you can stay on the sidelines and let them talk. Second, it shows that you pay attention to others' needs, and people will recognize that.

Remember, this is about baby steps. I'm not telling you to dive into a room full of strangers, only to feel like you've completely blown it and never want to go to an event again. It's essential for you to get what I refer to as "small wins," the good experiences that motivate you and that you can build on.

DON'T HIT THE ROCK!

Whether you're going to a business event, running a 5K, attending a fundraising event, or volunteering at your children's school, you're going to be around people. That means opportunities for connections. If introverted tendencies take over, remember that it's just your current comfort zone causing a little discomfort. The key is to set your intention before you go.

For example, your intention might be just to make one good connection. You can set a more specific intention, like making a connection that leads to a business opportunity for you or for someone else. Or maybe your intention is to connect to someone who can provide a resource that you need or can simply help you get information. A business opportunity doesn't just mean that the focus is sales. We're talking about connections.

Once you have your intention set, then it's time for what I call a mindfulness moment. The definition of mindfulness is the process of actively noticing new things, being aware of your experiences in the moment. Being mindful even for just a few minutes can change how you react to what's happening around you, and that includes getting your head in the connecting game.

If you've had one of those crazy-busy days with non-stop meetings, no time for lunch, and traffic jams in between, you might be saying to yourself, "This isn't going to be a good event." I can guarantee that you are not going to get the result that you want with that mindset because you've set yourself up for failure as a result of phenomenon called negativity bias.

Your mind reacts to bad things more quickly, strongly and persistently than to equivalently good things. This is really important if you're being chased by a lion. In fact, focusing on perceived threats is what kept human beings alive as hunter-gatherers, when we were always on the alert for danger. This is the reason that we have stressful, instantaneous fight-or-flight responses.

Today, it isn't lions triggering your fight-or-flight response. It's your cell phone ringing, your looming deadlines, your sick child, and other stressors that keep your focus. The way the mind works is that you're drawn toward what you think about. If you're playing golf and are focused on the pond you have to play around, you might not be surprised when you drive the ball right to it. For those of you who have kids, think back to when they were learning to ride a bike. There's something in the road—maybe a rock—and you yell, "Don't hit the rock!", what do they do? Smack right into it!

Research shows that you have to hold a positive thought in your field of attention for 10 to 20 seconds in order for that experience to make it into our long-term memory. Otherwise, the experience simply slips away. I don't mean that if you simply think positively all the time, life will be easy and you'll have everything you've ever wanted. Getting in the right mindset is about getting the results you want by taking the time to be aware of and—if need be—shifting what you're focusing on. Holding positive thoughts encodes positive experiences into long-term memory and focuses your energy less on the negative and more on the positive. And because the brain often sees what it expects to see, you'll make connections or you won't because of your focus.

So now that you've taken a moment to get your focus in the right place, it's time to plan. What I mean by that is that you should plan how you will walk into the event, how long you're going to stay, and how you're going to leave gracefully. On occasion, you may get into a wonderful conversation and may want deviate from your plan so you can stick around for a while. But if you're feeling nervous, take a few moments by yourself off to the side of the room or even the bathroom. This temporary break for mindfulness will help you get you refocused and (get back to your) plan.

Remember, connecting is about being strategic about your time and whom you want to meet. You don't have to end a conversation that's going well just because you want to stick to your plan. There could be an opportunity sitting right next to you. Opportunities can happen when you least expect them. And you'll be better able to recognize those good opportunities when you've got a positive mindset.

YOUR MENTAL FILTER

Watching others go from wallflower to connector gave me the confidence to know that I could do it, too. But it got even easier when I learned how creating those connections with people truly starts in the mind. This is because of a mental filter we have called the Reticular Activating System (RAS). The RAS acts like a filter on your subconscious mind. It sorts out important visual information that needs to be paid attention to from what is unimportant and can be ignored.

For a time, I sat on a non-profit board whose focus was working with at-risk girls in the Kansas City, Kansas, school district. I was gaining more confidence in my networking skills, and having to raise funds for the non-profit pushed me further outside my comfort zone. I jokingly say that if you're in fundraising, it means you're going to be kissing a lot of frogs. That's what it takes to get to the right donors. Fundraising puts you in a position to be rejected , but I found that when I asked for someone else, the rejection was much easier to deal with.

One evening in 2008, I was out with a friend at happy hour. The guy next to us at the bar looked like Bono from U2. We smiled but never spoke. When he went into the restaurant, my curiosity got the best of me, so I asked the waitress who he was. She told me his name was Mark and he was in the petroleum business. Immediately, that *Ding, ding, ding, money!* alarm went off in my head. (As a fundraising chair, you're always listening for those money signs.) It was my RAS at work!

About a month later, I was having a business breakfast at another restaurant, and Mark was there. I could see that he was looking at me with that look of, I think I know you but I'm not quite sure from where. Once again, we didn't talk. About a month later, I was having happy hour again with some former co-workers, and Mark was there. He walked up to me and said, "I think I've met you." I said, "No, but we've seen each other before at happy hour and breakfast."

Mark was there with a gentleman who was a cousin of a restaurateur whom I wanted to meet. I knew the restaurateur could be a great resource for our organization, so I asked Mark if he would introduce me to his friend, and he asked me why. I told him that I was the fundraising chair for a local non-profit that works with at-risk girls and that I was always looking for people who wanted to donate to our organization and who would be great resources for us.

Mark said, "Well, I'll give you money." And I said, "Great! I'll take $10,000." He had a stunned look on his face and I wasn't sure that he heard me so, of course, I repeated, "Really, I'll take $10,000."

He got quiet and I said, "Mark, give me your card. I'll call you Monday," which I did. I found out that, yes, he donated to a number of organizations, including youth charities. So I sent him information, and when we met a week later, he wrote me a check on the spot for $3,500.

After that meeting, Mark told me, "There's this guy that you need to meet. His name is Brad. He and his buddies have started a foundation that holds charity golf tournaments and donates the proceeds to other local charities in Kansas City."

When I called Brad, he said, "What great timing you have! We're just now in our selection process." So I sent him information about our organization and connected him to our executive director. That year, Brad's organization picked our charity and another local charity as the beneficiaries of their golf tournament, and we got a check for $15,000.

That whole experience showed me the power of asking. You never know who's in your network and who can lead you to the next person. Even if the person you're asking can't help, there is always one more question to ask (possibly the most important): "Do you know anyone who may be able to help with this?" You would be amazed at how many doors this simple question will open up. Depending on your network, you could be just two degrees from the person you need to meet.

I've shared this story in keynotes and private client events. Inevitably, someone says, "There's no way I could ever do that." At one time, I didn't think I could, either. This is when taking a moment to reflect on why you want to make connections is important. If someone else is telling you that you have to do it, your motivation will be slim. I was passionate about the organization so that helped in taking the pressure off of me. It wasn't an overnight process to shift my old mindset. I started with small steps to create new habits. Being mindful of my thoughts was a big part of it. I also discovered that when I set goals for who I wanted to meet and the resources that would be helpful, they seemed to show up. It wasn't magic but my RAS filtering through the 400 billion bits of information. Once I saw a connecting opportunity, then I had a choice to say nothing or to introduce myself. I started getting into a pattern: See the person and introduce myself, see the person and introduce myself. One day my mental lightbulb turned on and I realized that I'd been doing this regularly and it was getting easier.

So think about this: if you haven't set goals for whom you want to meet, then you're going to have a harder time recognizing or identifying people, opportunities, situations, and resources that could be helpful to you.

So that's why keeping your RAS tuned in is such a critical part of getting your head in the game with connecting. Who is that one person you want to meet or that resource you need? You won't find them at your desk in your office, you need to get out to make connections.

ONE SIZE DOESN'T FIT ALL

It helps to know when you're at your best. If you're not a morning person because you tell yourself every day that you're not a morning person, then attending a 7:00 a.m. networking event is probably not going to put you in the best mindset for making the best connections.

Extroverts love to be out. Extroverts love to be with people. If you're an introvert, you're going to have to apply a little bit more brain power, more cognitive effort, to making connections. It may feel like you have to psych yourself up to meet your own connecting goals, so don't overburden yourself. If you're tired after having a nonstop day, you have the choice to say, "OK, I'm going to take a minute to be mindful and plan. Whom do I want to meet when I get to the event, and is my mindset focused on good outcomes?" or "Is this just another one of those events I'm doing so I can check 'networking' off my list for the week?" It's this response that makes networking feel inauthentic, like it's just another thing you have to do because you're in business. Think about what you think about.

As wonderful as spontaneous connections can be, we don't have control over when a networking event is scheduled, unless we're the ones scheduling it. However, we do have control over other activities in our schedule.

Blocking activities together can help you to focus. For example, I'll book my schedule with back-to-back meetings for a couple of days a week, if I don't have to be out of town for a client. To balance those blocks, I schedule an office day to catch up and complete deliverables. I do the same for creative days, when I'm working on new projects. I don't schedule events out on those days because I want to be 100 percent focused on the tasks at hand. When I say event, I'm not just referring to a networking event. These could be wine club events or sporting activities, for example.

The extroverted folks—the people who are already comfortable being out among other people all the time—may not have a need for blocking. They may be just fine with a full schedule and events every night. My scheduled looks like an extrovert's schedule sometimes, but after the fourth event in one week, the introvert in me takes over and I am at tilt. I want to be at my best when interacting with people, so when I hit my own limits now, I can recognize them and plan a schedule that works better for me.

If you're an introvert and you've scheduled several super-busy days in one week, then you need to clarify what you need to do for each networking event in order to keep your mindset focused on the positive. Pay attention to your self-talk before the event, during the event, and before you walk up to a group of people. You'll set yourself up for failure by saying, "I'm not going to make any good connections. I know how these networking events are. It's never worth the time." It's negativity bias in action, and you get the results you focus on, so pay attention to your mindset.

This isn't a one-size-fits-all process. Part of it is finding the strategy that works for you. If you find yourself being reluctant to go to events, then tell yourself, "You know what? Instead of having to attend 10 events, I'm going to attend one." And then find a small group and see what it's like. The group could be focused on business or on special interests like book clubs, or gardening clubs. If sports is one of your interests, you could join a Facebook group to connect with folks who share your interest. As part of your connecting strategy, think about being the business and social events you attend as a chance to learn new things and have fun in ways that aren't socially demanding.

When you're planning to attend an actual networking event, set a clear time frame. Stay only 20 minutes or 30 minutes, and give yourself permission to leave as long as you accomplish that goal that you set, which could simply be having a conversation with one person. Or if it's just a completely uncomfortable situation, don't force yourself to stay. Giving yourself permission to leave can also help you to overcome a reluctant attitude if you've been avoiding going to events so you don't get overwhelmed. Remember, the point isn't necessarily to set an arbitrary goal, like talking to 15 people. The point is to go to an event and feel like you belong. Again, if you happen to be having a good time, give yourself permission to stay longer, too.

No matter what, don't pretend to be someone you're not. If you're an introvert, you don't have to act like an extrovert. That's not what developing connecting strategies that work for you is about. It's about helping you to get comfortable in your own skin and then find the approach that works best for you and where you're at right now in your career.

THAT NEW GUY

If you're new to "networking," remember that it's important to take baby steps. The more often you have a conversation or attend an event, the more you stretch your comfort zone. The more connections you make, the easier it gets to make more. It's all a process, and it takes time to create great relationships. I've been doing this since 2005, and when I started, I was lousy at networking. So the fact that you're reading the book means that you're already light-years ahead of where I was when I started. You're getting your process down. Taking time to plan your best approach will help you expand your comfort zone one step at a time.

As you're making the move to becoming a connector, look for ways that to push yourself outside of your comfort zone. You want to do things that scare you but don't paralyze you. And, finally, keep in mind that at every event, there are many other people who also feel like they're completely out of their comfort zones and would rather be anywhere but there. Instead of thinking about the situation negatively, follow the suggestion I offered in my book *Just Another Leap*: before you leap, focus on the small action steps that you can take as you work toward connecting success.

ACTION

Choose the top three things from chapter three that you feel are most important to your connecting advantage strategy. Take action on your Fast Start item now.

Fast Start

One-Hour Win

Snail It

CHAPTER 4

SERENDIPITY, CHANCE ENCOUNTERS, AND NINE CONNECTIONS IN TWO HOURS.

Tony Hsieh, the CEO of Zappos, spoke at Techonomy 2013 about the importance of increasing your collision rate—how often you interact with other people—in order to have more serendipitous encounters. According to *Forbes*, Hsieh helped build Zappos' brand by emphasizing community among his employees, inviting their input about what new social opportunities they might want to have as part of their Las Vegas offices. The employees requested a dog park, which Hsieh recognized as a place where employees built community naturally by colliding with their coworkers.

Collisions happen when you're literally out in your community. Opportunities are everywhere if you're willing to step outside your proverbial box of where you think connections can happen. The key is to make them happen. Such encounters can connect you with new people and new ideas and maybe even inspire your next leap. Your RAS can speed up your rate of serendipitous encounters. When you know what you're looking for, the right people will appear. Making connections starts with your intention. Pay attention to what you're thinking before heading out for the day.

COFFEE SHOPS AND ONLINE DATING

Great collisions can happen at events, at coffee shops, at your children's baseball practices, and even via online dating. Yes, you read that correctly: online dating. I dove into the online dating world several years back. (To be clear, I haven't been online in quite some time, so you won't find me on that social platform.)

At the time, I was looking to make connections for a client I was working with. We were looking specifically for individuals with a focus in venture capital or private equity as well as individual investors to provide $40 million in funding for this particular project. My RAS was highly tuned into those keywords. The words jumped out in LinkedIn profiles and business articles, and I had even overhead them in conversations happening around me. Because connecting is my business, I viewed dating profiles differently. I was open to the fact that if I met someone online as a potential date, there might also be an opportunity to connect about business. When reading someone's LinkedIn profile, you'll see off to the right where it shows the "People also viewed" column. These are often individuals who are in a similar industry or connected to those who are. The online dating site I was on had a similar setup, with additional profiles at the bottom. On dating sites, I was looking for people who had a specific age range close to my own age and who also had a background in business. One night, I was looking through profiles on the dating site, and one of the profiles that popped up at the bottom of my screen was of a guy who happened to fall slightly outside my criteria, based on what he was looking for. He was very detailed in his profile and had listed keywords that showed that he was in the financial world.

I immediately recognized him as being a potential connection for my client, even if he wasn't a potential dating connection for me. Having that mindset of being open to finding any kind of connection on the dating site—whether that connection might be to a new friend, colleague, client, or date—took the pressure off and made it easier to reach out to him to form a business connection. Isn't connecting what's important in the end, really?

When I reached out to him, it specifically intended to talk business only. I sent him an email and said, "Hey, it doesn't look like we're a fit for dating, but I would appreciate the chance to have coffee and a conversation to talk business." I'm sure that he was completely shocked to get this message. He replied back a few days later to say, "Yes, let's meet." Considering this wasn't the norm for making a business connection, I knew he wanted to research me as much as I did him, so we traded contact information, including our LinkedIn profiles. It just so happened that we had 11 connections in common on LinkedIn. Of course! The result of the meeting was the creation of a solid business relationship. In fact, he made several introductions to individuals in financial and investment services who reviewed my client's executive summary. The funding eventually came from another source, but these new connections were still of value. He became a tremendous resource for several individuals within my network, and a few deals closed as a result. In return, they were able to make beneficial introductions for him as well.

That was one of four stellar business connections I made via that online dating site. I was able to open numerous doors for one connection in the technology industry. Another connection referred me to a speaking engagement. The last connection I made reached out to me with the intent to talk business. Considering that he sold his company for $100 million, it was a nice thought that he felt I might be of assistance in some way. I guess what goes around comes around.

When I say that opportunities are everywhere, I really mean it. When your RAS is tuned in and you're willing to get out of your comfort zone to make the ask you need to make, you can get great results just like I did in getting Mark's donation and the golf tournament for the non-profit I worked with.

CHANCE ENCOUNTERS

Serendipity is what happens when you make fortunate discoveries by accident. You may be surprised to learn that you don't have to wait for serendipity to happen. You can *make* it happen.

When you schedule a meeting with someone else, try to get out of the office. You never know who else you'll run into. Coffee shops, restaurants, and hotel lobbies can be ideal for this. If you're an entrepreneur who tends to work alone or you office from home, it's easy to get caught up being in the office. Yes, a quiet space is ideal if you're working on deliverables for a client and need to be completely focused. But there are times when you need to be out because it will increase your chance to experience serendipitous encounters.

If you're someone who is easily distracted, then find a quiet corner. Set a time limit. Maybe schedule a few hours a week out of your office. It doesn't have to be a something you do every day. Remember, getting out equals meeting new people.

If you have a usual spot, you may notice that you keep seeing the same people time and time again. Think of it as connecting déjà vu. There was a guy I would often see at my usual hotel lobby meeting spot. His hair was grey and spiked; he was slender, and he always wore skinny blue jeans, a t-shirt, and sport coat. Looking at him, you might think he had retired from a rock-and roll-band. He always sat by himself, drinking coffee and reading his paper. My curiosity got the best of me, so I asked the folks at the front desk if they knew who he was. They said no, but they'd given him the nickname Rod Stewart. It fit! The funny thing was that I had a meeting at a coffee shop in another part of town later that day, and there he was. Those who know me well know that I have an insatiable curiosity, and I got over my fear of talking to strangers a long time ago, so I introduced myself. Turns out that "Rod" did play in a rock band in his former years! His son is also in a band now, so when he's not on the road with them, he hangs out, drinks coffee, and reads his paper. In this case, it wasn't a business connection, just a cool connection.

Speaking of connecting déjà vu, have you ever just happened to run into someone you know and had that person say, "You were on my mind"? Be sure to ask what made that person think of you. Or have you been out and run into someone you're friends with on Facebook but haven't gotten to meet yet in person? That happened to me on a business trip recently. I was at the airport checking in my luggage, and the guy behind me in line pulled out his phone, went to my personal Facebook page, and asked me, "Are you *this* Joyce Layman?"

You never know where the right place and right time will happen, so always be prepared for chance encounters. Don't forget to keep business cards on you because those connections could be more valuable than you think.

NINE CONNECTIONS IN TWO HOURS

I am truly blessed to have terrific people in my network who get what connecting is about. Mindy Hager is one of those people. She reached out to introduce me to a woman who was in a career transition. Over the course of her career, this woman had been a chief marketing officer for several companies in a niche market. She was looking to shift to another industry and wanted to expand her connecting opportunities. When she made the introduction, Mindy said, "You really need to meet Joyce because she knows a lot of people, and I think she could help you expand your connections."

For our first meeting, I picked Parisi, a local coffee shop in Kansas City, for two reasons. First, I love their coffee, and second, it's my favorite collision spot since I know the odds of running into other people are high when I'm there. The planets must have been aligned that day because I even surprised myself. In just two hours, nine people were there and four of them were great connections for her. It was easy to make introductions because of where we were sitting. There's a long counter when you walk in the door. At one end, they make your coffee order, and at the other end you can sit on stools at a bar-height counter. Smaller tables span the rest of the floor space. At 9:00 a.m. on a Friday morning, it was absolutely packed. I got there before she did and chose to sit at the counter. This put us in line with both of the coffee shop's doors.

Now, here's the thing. When you're meeting with somebody, you don't want to have darting eyes. You need to maintain eye contact with that person because, frankly, it's rude if you're talking to somebody but looking everywhere else. Out of my peripheral vision, I could see when people were coming in, so I could still maintain eye contact with her. When someone I knew walked by, I got the opportunity to reach out and say, "Hey, I'd like to introduce the two of you."

Introductions like the ones I made that day don't have to be complicated. It's simply a matter of introducing each person and describing in a few sentences what each of them do and the people they're looking to meet. If you know them well, then also include why you feel they benefit by knowing each other. I always suggest exchanging contact information. If for any reason someone doesn't have a card, then I make sure the connection happens via email. Get good at making introductions for other people when you're out and happen to see someone else you know. This is one way to create serendipity for others.

LOCATION, LOCATION, LOCATION

Because I'm one of those folks who offices from home, I take advantage of a variety of spots around Kansas City to hold meetings. I jokingly call Parisi my south office because I live on the other side of town. I have picked out strategic "office" locations around town based on the kind of meeting I'm having.

Consider the purpose of the meeting. If this is a high-level discussion, then you're going to want to be focused. Know the space you're meeting in, because some are ideal for carrying on a conversation but others are more difficult. For example, if you're a wealth adviser, banker, or attorney, and you're discussing confidential information, then the meeting should be held at your office or someplace that provides privacy. I'm surprised at how often I've overheard conversations that weren't appropriate for a public place. If the conversation doesn't have to be confidential, however, then you have lots of options.

Look at other ways that you can increase your collision rate and give yourself the opportunity to create serendipity for other people. Remember, this isn't always about business. This is about having quality conversations to enhance your relationships in the right environment.

SIX DEGREES OF KEVIN BACON

In 1929 Hungarian author Frigyes Karinthy, published several short stories about the idea that any two people can be connected by five people or fewer in their social network. The idea that each of us is only separated from any other person by just a few other people was tested in 1967 by social psychologist Stanley Milgram. In his experiment, Milgram sent letters to people in five cities in the U.S. and asked them to find the address for a specific person in Boston and send that person a letter. If the recipient of the letter from Milgram didn't know the addressee in Boston personally, the recipient was asked to send a letter to someone whom they knew personally and who they thought might know the person in Boston.

On average, letters passed through the hands of five to six people before a letter finally arrived at the right address in Boston. The results of the research were disputed because of poor follow-up with people in the social chains who had received letters. (How are *you* following up with your contacts?)

Fast forward to 2001, when Duncan Watts, a professor at Columbia University, recreated the study using email. Watts found the average of connections was, in fact, around 6.

A group of students at Albright College in Pennsylvania created a game out of the concept of six degrees of separation using the actor Kevin

Bacon as the target connection. The goal of the game is to link any actor to Kevin Bacon through no more than six connections. In the game, connections were determined by whether any two actors in the connection chain have appeared in a movie or commercial together. Kevin Bacon was probably chosen for this game because he's been in a lot of movies with a lot of different people, so it's easy to connect him with other actors. If you want to try the game for yourself, you can even find a few "six degrees of Kevin Bacon" calculators online.

I bet there are people you know personally who are a lot like Kevin Bacon: they seem to be connected to everyone. So why does this matter? In a word: relationships. If you can nurture and maintain relationships with the right people who can help you reach your personal, career, and business goals, you will thrive.

The good news is that you are truly six (or fewer) degrees of separation away from anyone you want to meet. You just need the right mindset in order to connect with them.

I do a "six degrees of Kevin Bacon" exercise when I'm facilitating events. And I'll tell you, I never cease to be amazed at the connections that happen when you get a room of people together. I've seen amazing connections happen in groups as small as 20 people and as large as 500 people. I always start by asking somebody to give me an example of a person as famous as Kevin Bacon, and then I ask the audience, "Do you know anyone who may have a connection to that person?"

These aren't necessarily direct connections, but we never fail to connect the dots once we turn our RAS to the celebrity in question. I've been in groups in which we've discovered connections to Denzel Washington, Bruce Springsteen, and Ina Garten, just to name a few. One of the best was a two-degree connection to Patti LaBelle. In a room of 50 people, one of the women present attended a church whose pastor was Patti LaBelle's cousin.

Once we've gone through this exercise, I take them through a follow-up exercise about connections to the companies and individuals they're looking to connect with. In a breakout session I was facilitating at a conference last July, someone was looking for connections to Fortune 50 leadership. It wasn't for a sale but for someone who could sit as an expert on a panel. In a room of 60 people, there were two people in the room who could make those introductions. Of course, a conversation would be needed to determine if this was the best introduction to make according to what they needed.

Your best connection to a resource can be sitting next to you at work, but if you don't share who or what company you want an introduction to, that connection may never happen. I once facilitated a program for business incubator in a small city. It was one of those cities where everyone literally knew everyone. There were about 50 people in the room for the program, and I took them through the "six degrees of Kevin Bacon" exercise to focus their RAS on finding connections to the individuals and companies they're targeting. After that, I asked for people to share the names of companies or individuals they wanted to meet. A woman raised her hand and shared the name of a company she wanted an introduction to. The guy sitting right next to her said, "I can make that introduction." My response: "Do you know each other?" They said, "Yes, we work for the same company." There were six people on staff in this company, yet the business developer hadn't reached out to ask for people to help her connect with these specific companies. Don't miss an opportunity for an introduction just because you didn't ask your closest connections how they can help.

Kansas City and the surrounding metro area has a population of 2.75 million. It's a big small city, and people who are connecting regularly know that it's typically one to two degrees of separation. What's your city or town like? The connecting strategy you create is going to depend on your city and the people you're looking to meet. Make a list of the people you would most like to meet—your top-connection list—and send out an email to the key people within your network to see if they can make an introduction. It may take a nudge to make that introduction happen, so be persistent.

A final note on six degrees and your personal brand. If you think you can do something in your business life that doesn't come out in your personal life, you will be surprised. In a place like Kansas City—where people seem to be separated by just one or two degrees—it's always amazing to see how quickly information travels and who knows about it. That's why you always want to be putting your best foot forward.

DECREASING DEGREES, INCREASING COLLISIONS

You can use social media to increase your collision rate online because with most social media, you're literally one degree away from people you want to meet.

Access to someone on social platforms varies depending on which platform you're using. Twitter gives you access to anyone whether they follow you back or not (as long as they haven't "protected" or hidden their tweets). The great thing about Twitter is that you can mention somebody in a tweet, like I did with the CEO of the technology company I wanted to meet. Mentioning him gave me a way to make an immediate connection.

Facebook's security settings are different. The ways that you can connect to people on Facebook depend on how they set their security settings. As mentioned before, usually, people have to accept your friend request before you can see the full details of their profile or "tag" (mention) them in a post. Check your settings. If you're in business, it's ideal to have them set so anyone can send you a friend request. Otherwise, you're missing potential opportunities.

LinkedIn gives you access to view people's profiles and view most of their detailed information, even if they're not among your "contacts" (like "friends" on Facebook). You can still send a message to people who aren't in your contacts, but you can't access their contacts lists. Like with Facebook, you can also mention people who're not in your contacts group, but the mention won't link to their profiles.

LinkedIn provides a plethora of content in several ways, including their LinkedIn Publisher posts and posts by Influencers. There are around 500 professionals specifically designated on LinkedIn as "Influencers." The list includes people like Richard Branson, Bill Gates, and Arianna Huffington. Influencers are invited to publish posts on LinkedIn about their work, cities, success, and business strategy. It's easy to repost great content through these LinkedIn features.

Keep in mind that when you share people's content on LinkedIn, your post will automatically link to their profiles (if you are connected) but not to their Twitter profiles. That's why when I want to share posts by LinkedIn Influencers, I also click the "Share Twitter" tab to make sure the posts get linked to their Twitter profiles and they can see that someone has been sharing their posts. On occasion, someone's Twitter profile won't show up in the link, so it takes an extra step to find the profile on Twitter and complete the post. People who don't have a Twitter profile or check their notifications regularly won't see the post, but your followers will.

MY NEW BEST FRIEND

One of the Influencers whom I was fortunate to come across on LinkedIn is Jeff Haden. Jeff has ghostwritten almost 40 books, four of them hitting #1 on Amazon's Business and Investing bestseller list. He's a contributing editor for *Inc. Magazine* and author of *TransForm: Dramatically Improve Your Career, Business, Relationships, and Life One Simple Step at a Time.* It's easy to see why he's got a massive following on LinkedIn and over 36,000 followers on Twitter. The posts that I see from Jeff on LinkedIn and Twitter are always relevant and thought-provoking.

Jeff noticed that I had been retweeting some of his posts, so he replied back on Twitter, "Appears you should be my new best friend." That got my attention! I was already sharing his posts, so—needless to say—this gave me even more motivation to reach out to him. In an effort to add value, I mentioned both Jeff and Bob Burg in the tweet and said, "If you don't know each other, you should." Of course, it turns out that they did already know each other, but the interaction opened the door for a brief conversation on Twitter among all three of us.

Define your goal for what you want to accomplish online. Write down a list of the people you currently have relationships with as well as the ones you want to develop relationships with. These could be Influencers, subject matter experts, clients, strategic connections, and more. Just because someone isn't local doesn't mean you won't have a chance to meet them in person. My connection with Bob Burg is a great example of that. What platforms are these people on? Connect with them either by following them or sending a customized request and start to develop those relationships. Chapter six will include some helpful templates for sending out those requests.

THE PLATFORM STRUGGLE

I've found that sometimes people don't get on social media platforms if they're uncomfortable with technology or don't see the value of the platforms. But this isn't about you. This is about the people you're looking to connect to. So I'm going to tell you gracefully: you're going to have to get over yourself and get out there, even if you're struggling to be comfortable with social media. I'm not saying that you have to get on every platform, but you need to be active on the ones that offer you the most value.

Twitter has been a terrific platform for making connections on many levels. If you think that Twitter is a waste of time, let me tell you a story: Several years ago, I was featured in John Maxwell's "A Minute with Maxwell," which is a daily email sent to his subscribers. A CEO who is also a fan of John's and one of his followers on Twitter started following me after he saw a tweet that John had tagged me in. Then he friended me on Facebook, even though we didn't have any mutual connections. I'll admit, the thought ran through my head: "Is this guy a stalker or friend of value?" But his profile photo was of him and his daughter, and I'm always open to making great connections and have learned not to prejudge, so I went ahead and accepted the friend request.

At the time, the CEO's company was experiencing significant changes that were out of their control. After reading some of my posts on Twitter and Facebook, he recognized me as someone who could potentially help his company, so he sent me an email through my website. The result was an engagement at which I spoke to his entire organization, and then I facilitated a two-day program for his leadership team as they put together a strategic plan. They needed to shift their thinking about the change and the opportunities ahead of them. And that's what I came in to help them do.

The CEO was able to recognize how I could help because I was consistent in my messaging on social media. Because we are both fans of John Maxwell, the CEO took notice of me, and we've been connected ever since. He started following me on Twitter because of John but continued to follow me because he connected to the content I was posting. Twitter—and social media in general—can be a valuable way to increase your collision rate. I post things that I feel are relevant to followers. Now, it's not that I don't get sidetracked on occasion by posting a feel-good story, but I know that everything I post speaks to my brand.

You may not be actively seeking out connections on LinkedIn or other social media platforms, but if you have a profile on the platforms that are most valuable to your brand, then you're increasing the opportunity to improve your collision rate. And when you're posting content of value, you're encouraging the people you collide with to make meaningful connections with you.

When you're looking to follow somebody, build the relationship one post at a time. You want to be a professional, not a stalker. If someone I don't know reaches out to me on LinkedIn but they have no photo, only a handful of connections, and very little information posted about themselves, I would immediately think, "I'm not so sure." However, I'll do a little bit of research on the person to find out to find out if we have any mutual connections, shared interests, or a similar professional background. If I think it will be a good connection to make, I'm happy to make the connection because, again, I want to connect with folks who believe in creating mutually beneficial valuable relationships.

No matter what you're posting on social media platforms, don't join conversations without doing a little bit of research first to make sure that what you're posting fits the context of the conversations you want to be part of. That's how you'll be able to define your value proposition to the people you want to connect with, by making sure that you're in the right place, contributing relevant content that provides value. Also, be careful not to spam folks on social platforms. It's happened numerous times to me, and I would suspect that you may have experienced comment-spam posts, too. Instead of adding to the conversation, the person posts a brief comment and a link to their website, which screams, "I'm desperate, please do business with me!" Be respectful and professional with what you share. Once you post something, it's hard to take it back, and deleting a post doesn't mean that your followers and friends didn't see it. People form first impressions quickly, so it's really important that you're putting your best foot forward by posting content of value when it's most valuable to post it.

EVENT COLLISIONS

You can increase your collision rate at events via social media. Once you find out who is presenting and whether you have an interest in their topic, do some research to find out what social media platforms they are on and then follow them. Before the event and at the event, retweet, and share their content. If you're the one speaking at an event, pay attention to who's reaching out to connect or to follow you. You can miss key opportunities by ignoring your new "fans," followers, and friends.

If there's a hashtag for the event—like #TEDxWomen or #TEDxKC—then use it in your posts. When you include a hashtag with your post, it's included in a searchable stream of tweets from other Twitter users who are also using that hashtag. There may also be hashtags for key words speakers use that are relevant to their brands. Now that *Your Connecting Advantage* is published, you can join in a conversation about the book and your progress using #YourConnectingAdvantage and #connectinghack.

It's always fun to watch that streaming conversation in real time because it gives you additional insight on what others are doing and thinking at the event. Seeing who's using hashtags will help you to see who else is in the audience that you may not be aware of. This is another valuable way to expand your relationships because other folks who see that you do the same things may want to connect, and you may want to connect with them, even if you don't know it yet.

The point of being at the event is to learn, so you may be limited on the time you can spend on social media. If you can't follow folks on Twitter immediately, for instance, then rely on the event hashtag to go back and find them. If you are able to follow somebody immediately, then you can use Twitter's list feature to sort those new connections into a list based on that event.

Twitter lists are a great way to keep track of top connections. Determine how you will organize your lists. It could be by specialty, by industry focus, lists of thought leaders, or groups of people with similar interests. Of course, you can put folks on multiple lists. Sorting people you follow into lists shortens the time you spend finding great content to retweet and folks to mention because it helps you narrow your focus to whatever the shared interests are of the people on your list. It helps you to have great conversations and add value.

ALL ABOUT BOB

Make sure you're genuine with your online connections. The key here is personal interactions, engaging with the folks you actually enjoy talking to when there isn't a financial gain. That's how I got to know Bob Burg.

For years, I've been one of Bob Burg's biggest fans. He's a speaker and national best-selling author not only of *Endless Referrals* and *The Go-Giver* but also of *Go-Givers Sell More* and *It's Not About You.* He's known as the ultimate connector, and he is my networking idol. You could call him the Peyton Manning of networking. He has an impressive network, including thought leaders like John Maxwell and Randy Gage. Years ago, when I didn't have a clue about how to network, I saw Bob give a keynote to an audience of 8,000 people at a conference, and I was just in awe of him.

Later, when I was making the shift from wallflower to connector, I decided to send Bob a direct message via Twitter to get his perspective on networking and mindset because I was doing a talk on that topic for a local leadership organization. I thought, "Why not ask? The worst that could happen is that he turns me down."

I was surprised to get a response from Bob within 15 minutes that said, "Absolutely! I'm happy to talk to you." He sent me his email address and said, "Email me your questions." After I emailed him the questions, he replied, "Great! I want to talk to you via phone." When we had the conversation—which was fantastic—Bob told me that he was going to be in Kansas City the following week.

The next week, in Kansas City, Bob spoke to an intimate group of about 30 people. After his presentation, Bob and I were able to get together and continue the conversation that we had started over the phone. A couple of years later, I invited Bob to Kansas City to speak at an event. I had the privilege of sharing the stage with him there, and I was able to make several key introductions for him.

It took courage to reach out to Bob via Twitter to ask for his insights. He could have said, "No, thanks," or he could have chosen not to reply at all. But it turns out that Bob is extraordinarily gracious, and I never would have known that if I hadn't taken the leap to contact him.

Think about how you can add value to someone you're connected to online. This doesn't need to be a grand gesture. It could easily just be answering a question in a LinkedIn group or contributing to a Twitter conversation. You can also be an online connector between other people. But be careful not to go overboard. It's great to mention someone in a Facebook post, but when someone is constantly mentioning or promoting somebody else, it can seem forced or even fake. It's easy to tell who's being genuine and who's just being annoying about over-promoting someone else. The point is to find a balance that adds value to your posts and the connections you make. Valuable posts will lead to a better collision rate.

#CONNECTINGHACK

Another great way to increase or create your own collision serendipity is to go to Quora or Stack Exchange or another popular question-and-answer site in your particular industry and answer two to three questions. This will show that you're knowledgeable in a particular subject and can be an easy way to associate your name with that subject without having to set up your own website or blog. And in some cases, the answers you post are more likely to be discovered and recognized than a blog post. The key is to put yourself online in ways that are going to help other people to notice you in a good way.

STRATEGIC SERENDIPITY

If there is a particular blog that you like to read, you can increase your collision serendipity by inquiring about contributing a guest post. If, for example, you've been invited to write for LinkedIn Publisher, then take advantage of that opportunity by posting regularly, even if it's once a month. You can also target online magazines about writing an article on a topic that is relevant to you. Writing for online magazines is a great way to add value to a publication that you like and promotes your interests, and it gives you an opportunity to build relationships with the magazine's editorial team. Do some research first to see which online magazines might be a good fit for your topic and writing style. If you're writing for a site that is well-known in your field and your post or article offers new insights, you'll be adding value and increasing your visibility as a thought leader on the subject. Just remember that if you don't ask, the answer will always be no.

As part of your strategy for creating new collision opportunities, you'll want to track where you're getting the most valuable results—new followers, higher numbers of comments or retweets, etc.—from what you post. Determine where your results are paying off and where they're not, because your time is worth money, and I want to ensure that you're being cognizant of that. You don't want to get to the end of a week or a month and feel that you completely wasted your time.

Ultimately, your connecting advantage is about relationships. Relationships are built on conversations, whether in person or via social media. Those conversations are incredibly powerful for helping you to expand your network. Thanks to social media, what would have taken you years to build can now be formed in a matter of months and sometimes even weeks.

"YES" VS. "YES BUT"

Woody Allen said that 80 percent of success is just showing up. So consider making a show-up rule. When you're invited, how often do you catch yourself saying, "Yes, but..." instead of just "Yes"? I'm not suggesting that you have to go to everything you're invited to or see on the calendar, because that approach may not be in line with your overall connecting strategy. You may be up against a deadline in your business or have a personal matter that requires a lot of your time. Consider what you have going on in your life and if any given event is a good use of your time based on whom you're looking to meet and what your needs are.

I have had numerous serendipitous moments at events that were outside my usual list of fundraisers, awards events, conventions, breakfasts, and other business events. Each of these opportunities opened doors to connections within new circles of influence. When you walk in, you may not know whom you'll find, but if you see it as a room full of opportunity, that's when the magic happens. That's your mindset staying focused on a positive result, not letting negativity bias affect you. You'll notice that a positive mindset tunes in your RAS and can increase your confidence, too, so that you can create more serendipitous collisions. My motto is: opportunities are everywhere.

Saying "Yes" instead of "Yes, but..." opens you up to new opportunities. And that's easy to do when you get stuck in a comfort zone. Saying "Yes" can create wonders when you're looking to make great connections.

Describing his research on luck, Professor of psychology Richard Wiseman explains that "lucky people generate good fortune via four basic principles. They are skilled at creating and noticing chance opportunities, make lucky decisions by listening to their intuition, create self-fulfilling prophecies via positive expectations, and adopt a resilient attitude that transformed bad luck into good."

Serendipity requires you to be open to new opportunities as you're moving along. Sometimes, you have to go out of your way to have new experiences and meet new people. Introverts might find this a little bit more difficult than extroverts. It's OK to take baby steps. But if you want new opportunities, then you're going to have to take those steps to get outside your comfort zones and increase your collision rate. The next chapter will cover your next step: looking for new events.

ACTION

We're there again and it's time to take action on your top three items from chapter four. Give yourself kudos for making it this far in the book because that is a big deal.

Fast Start

One-Hour Win

Snail It

CHAPTER 5

HIT-AND-RUNS, CARD COUNTERS, AND A WINGMAN

If you've been wondering, "When will Joyce give us the scoop about what to do at a networking event?", your wait is over. It's time to get strategic about where and with whom you're going to be spending your time.

Too often, I see people going to networking event after networking event wondering why they're not getting the results they're looking for. They show up with the intention of handing out their cards to as many people as possible, hoping to make an easy sale. Or they think that a quick conversation gives them permission to ask people they've just met to make connections for them. Or they assume that showing up to talk with the same people they already know means they're networking effectively. But going to a lot of networking events doesn't necessarily make you a great networker. It just makes you super-busy.

TIME REALLY IS MONEY

You've probably heard the expression that time is money. Try this brief exercise to calculate what your time is actually worth. You can also do the calculations based on what you'd like to earn or any raises or increases in business that you anticipate. I'm not looking for a highly detailed answer, like personal-finance guru Dave Ramsay might want from you. This should be just a snapshot of the value of your time.

1. What was your actual income last year?

2. On average, how many hours a week do you work?

3. Take the number of hours a week x 50 weeks (2 included for vacation or personal time off). *Example:* 40 hours a week x 50 weeks = 2000 hours

4. Divide your income by the total number of hours worked to determine what an hour of your time is worth.

Are you surprised at the result? Seeing how much an hour of your time is worth can help you gauge the cost of attending a networking event. Don't forget to calculate the driving time to and from the event itself, since that's costing you time as well. The city you live in will affect your event strategy. It's fairly easy to get around in Kansas City, even when there's rush hour traffic, whereas if you live in Los Angeles, Washington D.C., or Chicago, the amount of time you spend commuting to an event on the other side of your city may or may not be worth your investment.

LOCATION, LOCATION, LOCATION PART 2

Your first step is to decide where to go. Start with targeting specific organizations and their events. Consider asking friends or colleagues for their best suggestions about organizations they've gotten the most value from, and keep a master list of those suggestions that you can go back to once you've checked them out for yourself.

You can start with an internet search on an organization's name. Read the fine print on the organization's website. Are the benefits of joining the organization clearly explained, and is there a forum for member feedback, comments, and interactions? Are there other social media platforms linked on the website that the organization uses regularly? You can look at the organization's activity on its Facebook page. Check to see if it has a YouTube channel and whether valuable content is being posted there. If the organization is on Twitter, do a quick skim of its tweets. Are these the kind of messages that you find of interest? Does the organization have a lot of followers, and are the followers tweeting about the organization? Are the conversations they're having ones you want to participate in? Be sure to check out what their followers are saying about the events that the organization holds and ask yourself if those events are ones you think you want to participate in.

You can also research key members—such as executive directors, board members, and event coordinators—and ask yourself whether they are the kind of people with whom you've been looking to build relationships.

My go-to organization in Kansas City is Central Exchange. It's been in existence for 35 years with two locations in the city and over 1000 members, including everyone from solopreneurs to people who work for large corporations, and offers more than 400 programs a year to support members in business development, leadership development, personal development, and special interests. Being a member at Central Exchange has opened the doors to many of my best business opportunities. The added bonus is that I've met some of my closest friends there, too. It's not just the programming but the culture that makes this my favorite organization to network in.

Which organizations should you consider checking out? Chambers of Commerce are always important to consider. So are civic and alumni associations. Think about professional associations and their conferences. Non-profit organizations and their fundraising events are also great places to make connections because you'll be talking to other folks who share the same passions.

You can also find social networking opportunities that aren't tied directly to business-focused organizations. Check out the events happening at country clubs, community centers, and local places of worship. Maybe there's a book club or a discussion group that meets at your favorite coffee shop. If you're more of a wallflower and the thought of walking into a happy hour where you don't know anyone makes you uncomfortable, then look for a more intimate event in a relaxed setting. It can help take some of the awkwardness out of it.

What social networking groups are in your city or town? You may want to consider using Meetup to find a group based on shared interests. Those of you who are interested in making connections in the entrepreneurial and start-up community might be interested in 1 Million Cups, which started in Kansas City and is now in numerous locations across the country. If you're more interested in volunteering and service, consider groups like Rotary International and Kiwanis International.

On occasion, I will make a "guest appearance" at a new networking group or special event, if it's under the right circumstances. Of course, I do my research beforehand so that I'm not going in blindly. If you're going to a new group or event, find out the purpose of the group and who could be there. Doing your research will help you choose the right places to network and help you focus your RAS on what you want once you're there, ultimately increasing the value of your collision rate. And if attending a new event makes you a little nervous, then arrive early. It's easier to walk into a room with a few people than a lot. Besides some of the best connections can happen before and after an event, like when you find yourself unexpectedly in a conversation in the parking lot.

#CONNECTINGHACK

There are a lot of great websites and apps that you can use to find out what's going on with social and networking events. A few examples include MyChamberApp and Meetup. If you're searching for a job, then consider trackers like JibberJobber that help you keep track of networking relationships as well as jobs you've applied to. If you're a Yahoo user, then check out XOBNI to manage your address book.

CONFERENCE CONNECTING

A common misconception is that conferences are places just to find insight. Conferences are good for many things, including providing a place to meet like minded people. These can be some of your best opportunities. The way to maximize your time at a conference (or convention) is to be a conference connector, not just an attendee. This means being prepared in advanced with a list and a few details about the people you want to meet. The more you fine-tune your list, the easier it will be to make the connections that you're looking for.

The term "serendipity accelerator" is used in social psychology circles to refer to what happens when we meet people in what we think are serendipitous circumstances. In fact—according to another psychological principle called the mere-exposure effect—what happens is that we tend to like things we're exposed to often. You've experienced this effect if you've seen the same commercial repeated over and over. The mere fact that you have been repeatedly exposed to that commercial increases your tendency to like the commercial and the product it advertises.

Your serendipity can seem to have accelerated when you're at conferences about things you're interested in. You just happen to sit next to people who are like minded or experiencing similar work challenges as you. They may be going to the same breakout sessions to gain insight on the interests or challenges you have in common. This gives you the opportunity to connect on a number of levels.

What makes it even better is when you discover you have mutual connections in common and, potentially, the chance to introduce each other to connections or resources that may be of assistance. If you're willing to get out of your comfort zone, you may end up continuing the conversation over coffee or dinner before the conference ends. Taking advantage of those opportunities to connect is going to enhance your serendipity.

NETWORKING OR SWEATWORKING

Fast Company published an article—"Networking is over. Welcome Sweatworking?"—about using the time you spend doing your favorite physical activities to connect with folks who also like doing the same activities. Often, going to the gym, being out on the golf course, running, cycling, or walking are opportunities to accomplish a couple of things at once: doing an activity that you enjoy and networking.

In fact, some companies offer structured "sweatworking" events so that fitness-conscious entrepreneurs and young professionals can meet and mingle. Some companies use their sweatworking events as recruiting tools to incentivize new talent to join the company. Some biotech companies in Los Angeles and San Diego reportedly hold weekly "board meetings" in the ocean, on surfboards, sometimes using the meetings not just for business but as a networking opportunities for bringing in different industries. Whether you're looking to build camaraderie among staff, establish rapport with a new business partner, land a new job, or simply try a new workout, sweating together can be a great equalizer that allow connections can grow in a new way.

"Location, location, location" has a whole new meaning in today's connecting world. Too many people think of connecting as schmoozing at a business event, even though the best connections can happen anywhere at any time. The whole point of your connecting advantage is to be purposeful about developing your strategy. Ask yourself what the best ROI for your time will be for going to a new networking event or trying out a new approach like sweatworking. Be willing to step out of your comfort zone for high-value opportunities.

PIGEONHOLES

I've noticed that some people limit themselves by limiting their connections to one particular group or organization. It's true that the more time you spend with individuals or groups of people, the more you learn about them and how they serve their clients and operate in life. If you're only in industry- or location-specific groups, then you limit yourself to making connections to the other people in those groups. Does being involved in those specialized groups mean that you're limiting your connections to people who are always going to be the best fit for you or for a potential introduction you want to make for someone else? Not necessarily.

When I'm looking at making business connections, I want to make sure that I'm aligning the best product and service with the best person to deliver it, as well as the best personality match for the individuals involved. The last thing I want to get is a phone call or email saying I didn't make a good introduction. For example, I know a dozen wealth advisors who prefer to work with particular types of clients based on the amount of the clients' investible assets, age range, and experience level with investments. I've taken the time to get to know the wealth advisors and their business models so that I know what the best fit will be.

For those of you who still say, "I'm not going to network with anybody outside of my group," then you could be missing out on significant connecting opportunities. Think of it this way: If you're a service professional who owns a lawn service company, for example, or a heating and cooling company or a or home-security company and you employ a variety of staff to deliver service to a large geographic area, you probably try to make sure there's a good personality fit between the staff you send out on a job and the clients they're serving. Not every staff member's personality will fit every client, and vice versa. The more diverse your staff, the more opportunity you'll have to work successfully with a variety of clients. If you're a solopreneur or have a company with a just a few key employees, it's imperative to have a business expertise fit as well as a personality fit between staff and clients or potential clients. The same goes for how you network: if you're trying new approaches at new events held by organizations you may not have interacted with before, the more you increase your collision rate and open yourself to new connecting opportunities.

An introduction means your reputation is on the line. There are really no excuses to limit your network. Think "best fit," and it's a win-win situation for all involved.

POWER POSING

Body language is an important part of a successful strategy for attending networking events. If you're nervous walking into an event, social psychologist and TED speaker, Amy Cuddy, suggests that power posing can increase your confidence. Simply standing in a confident pose or holding your hands above your head like you're celebrating a win can influence your brain chemistry and your attitude in positive ways. Even though I've been speaking since 2008, I take a few minutes to do a power pose before every keynote to help me get centered and focused. It's part of the mindfulness process that I use regularly.

As I mentioned in chapter one, it takes a tenth of a second for someone to form a first impression about you from your photo. We also form first impressions based on a person's tone of voice and posture. Body language has four times the impact that verbal does. Goldfish-like attention spans and information overload from the 400 billion bits of information we process every second also influence this impression. You may only get one chance to make an impression, so make it a great one! This goes both ways, as some folks who're only at networking events to sell and not to make mutually beneficial connections aren't worth getting to know. These are the "takers," and they are fairly easy to spot because you'll notice that the entire conversation is about them. They don't ask questions about you and your business. It just feels inauthentic. It's almost like they have giant neon signs on their foreheads that say "Buy from me." Make that judgment once you have more information. This is not about putting on a different persona. It's about being genuine and putting your best foot forward.

Sometimes, it's how you looked when you said something, not what you actually said. Ray Birdwhistell, an anthropologist who led the first studies of nonverbal communication, estimated that we can recognize 250,000 facial expressions. Looking nervous is certainly going to come across to the person you're talking to. If there is a conflict between what you say and your non-verbal clues, the person you are talking to is more likely to disbelieve your words.

Allan and Barbara Pease, internationally renowned experts in human relations and body language and authors of *The Definitive Book of Body Language*, conducted research that found that body language comprises 60 to 80 percent of communication in negotiations and 60 to 80 percent of people form an initial opinion about someone in under four minutes. Their research also indicated that when negotiations were made on the phone, the stronger argument won, but negotiations made in person were heavily influenced by the gestures and body language of the people at the negotiating table.

SWEATY PALMS AND LIMP WRISTS

Your handshake is critical for making a great first impression. A networking event isn't the WWF, so pinching or gripping someone's hand to the point it's uncomfortable is just as bad as a weak, limp handshake or the dreaded sweaty-palms handshake. I wear rings on my right hand and have experienced what I call crushing-grip handshakes far too often. Maybe you have, too. Ever had someone shake your hand and not let go for what seemed like an eternity? The other side of this is the flash: it's so quick, you don't know that it actually happened. These all leave an impression, and depending on whom you're greeting, it may not to be a good one.

Then there are the times when you walk out of the bathroom and your hands are damp either because the towels aren't there or the dryer didn't work the way it should, and somebody walks up to you with a hand extended. Been there myself. It's better off to let that person know your hand is damp and give the option to shake or not to shake than to have to apologize afterward.

The ultimate handshake fail happens during cold and flu season. If you have a cold, please let the other person know. If you're not feeling good, say so. Even the best connectors need to do an occasional elbow tap as an alternative to a handshake. Regardless of the situation, if something went wrong with your handshake, simply say, "That wasn't the proper handshake. Let's try that again."

Also, be aware of cultural differences with handshakes. I was at an event recently where the keynote speaker was from Japan. I went to introduce myself afterwards. Instead of a handshake, he put his palms together and gave a slight bow. As an American from the Midwest, I feel pretty comfortable shaking everybody's hands and maintaining eye contact, even with strangers. I didn't know that trying to shake his hand could have been a giant faux pas. So be aware of cultural differences. Try to do some research about possible cultural differences before attending an event where you are likely to interact with people from other cultures. It's just part of what it takes to make a great impression.

DON'T JUDGE ME

Judging people based on their professions or job titles could mean missing fabulous opportunities. If you're not connecting with people because your first impression of what they are wearing, saying, or even acting like doesn't fit what you think is OK, then you fall into the category of people who aren't thinking beyond the first tenth of a second. The person you're talking to could just be a client's friend, spouse, or significant other who happens to be at the event but isn't comfortable in that situation. You never know who you're talking to, so do not judge too quickly. Make sure you get enough information before you formulate your judgments because it takes a lot to change that mindset.

And then there are those who attend but may not see the value in the event. Once when I was attending a Chamber coffee at Dean & Deluca, I noticed a guy standing next to a column by himself with his arms crossed. I recognized this wallflower body language because I used to use it, too. Of course, I approached him and discovered he had recently sold his company but stayed on as the Director of Business Development in order to maintain the relationships he had built with mega-clients over the years. He told me that no one in the room was a good connection for him because he was used to dealing with the Sprints and AT&T's of the world. I love a good challenge and knew that I could change his mind. After meeting that day, I sent him a copy of Bob Burg's *The Go Giver* in the hopes that it would provide him with new insight about connections.

A year later, this individual came upon an investing opportunity that he couldn't pass up, but he needed connections to venture-capital, private-equity, and individual investors to take advantage of the opportunity. At the time, I had distant connections to individuals through my network who could help him. I researched possible introductions I could make for my client to my established connections, including the guy I'd connected with through online dating and who I knew could make introductions to secure $40 million for a project. Then I continued my research on LinkedIn, and ultimately I was able to open up a whole new world of connections for my investment client. Needless to say, my client changed his mind about making preemptive judgments.

The person in the corner may be shy or feeling out of place, but that person could also be the next tech whiz. I was at an outdoor concert recently and my friend Dawn was there with me. It was 85 degrees in the middle of the afternoon, and I noticed a teenage girl walking by wearing a grey sweatshirt with black horizontal stripes and a hood that had ears like a fox. I pointed her out to Dawn. She said, "That's my neighbor's daughter. She has a thyroid issue and is always cold." It turns out that this young lady is a 13-year-old tech whiz. She already has clients who contract with her to build apps. You never know what great opportunities to connect might walk right by you if judge before you before you get to know someone.

As Jeff Haden said in his *Inc. Magazine* article "10 Habits of Remarkably Polite People":

> "They never judge. They don't judge the person they are speaking to. They don't judge other people. They don't judge other cultures or countries or, well, anything. Why? Remarkably polite people realize they aren't perfect either."

Wise words!

MASTERING THE ART OF SOCIAL JIUJITSU

I won't share everything Jeff writes about in that article (because you need to follow him and read his articles), but I do have to mention one part that caught my eye: remarkably polite people are masters of the art of social jiujitsu. Jeff defines social jiujitsu as "the ancient art of getting you to talk about yourself without you ever knowing it happened."

As one who is insatiably curious, I enjoy hearing people's backstories, what got them started down the career paths they are on, transformational moments in their lives and careers, the influencers they follow, the books they read, etc. It's about simply asking questions, as Jeff says, "the right questions." Getting to know someone isn't being manipulative. It's having a meaningful conversation to find mutual connecting points. Too often, people get caught up on the conversation of business and forget it's the personal connection that matters most. People need to know who you are and what you stand for. If they like you and trust you, it opens doors for a relationship, whether business or personal.

STRANGER DANGER

It dawned on me one day that I wasn't really a wallflower. I was just uncomfortable in a networking situation because I wasn't quite sure of what to do or say. I could easily have conversations with my clients, co-workers, friends at the stable where I kept my horse, etc. They were once strangers, too. And I also assumed that networking meant being on the receiving end of a pushy, three-foot rule approach, and that was inauthentic. Ultimately, my perception of what networking was supposed to be and how badly I was failing at it were the reasons I was a wallflower.

The idea of "stranger-danger" that you may have learned as a kid might still bring out your nerves, so practice pushing your comfort zones before you go to a formal event. You can do this by having a brief conversation with someone the next time you go to the grocery store, the next time you're standing in line for the restroom, or while you're waiting for a class at the gym to start. You're only going to be there a few minutes, so your risk is low. Compliment the person standing next to you. Ask that person about how the day is going. It's brief conversations like this that will increase your confidence at an actual networking event.

If you're willing to expand the experience, then consider volunteering on a committee, at your place of worship, or in a special interest group. This gives you a chance to get to know people in an interesting setting that doesn't focus on business. Another option is be the person at a networking event's registration table. It's a quick conversation, you'll get to meet a lot of people, and you can start to see who's connecting with whom.

If you're completely frozen at an event, the event organizers and the people who are checking everyone in are your best allies. This is where having your logline ready is going to help others to understand who you are and who a great connection would be for you. Even if you don't have your logline ready, you can simply introduce yourself and let them know you're a little nervous (you're probably not the only one). Ask them who they feel would be great people to talk to and if they would introduce you. Brilliant conversation starters are in the next section, so hold on for more ideas.

Remember, a conversation doesn't always have to be business-focused. A coaching client of mine was new to the area, and even though she was in relationship development for her company, her primary interest was connecting with other moms who could provide insight on the resources for her kids.

You could be the one who has the resources—like a book or an article—that other people are looking in their areas of interest. A resource I love sharing with people is TED talks. I spoke at TEDxUMKC and am always interested to find out what TED talks other people enjoy and have found helpful, both professionally and personally. I can then point other folks to those TED talks for insights and inspiration.

ICE BREAKERS...

No matter what event you go to, *somebody* has to get the party started.

I was at a fundraising lunch event recently. There were table sponsors for all but three tables, which didn't have any signs and were considered open seating. I noticed there were four people at one of the tables and one guy sitting by himself at the next table over.

I walked up to the group of four people and said, "Is this the fun table?" That immediately broke the ice and got an a unanimous "Of course it is" from everyone seated. Truly, would anyone say no to that question? They turned out to be a really fun bunch of people with great conversation skills. Being a former wallflower, I turned around to the guy who was by himself at the next table and said, "Why don't you come over and join us?" He did and said he appreciated the invitation.

If you're the one with the more extroverted personality, then be the connector who gets people engaged at an event or even at a table.

Introverted or wallflower types have a harder time doing that and will appreciate your taking the lead.

When sitting at a table or even in a one-on-one conversation, pick a topic of general interest. Is there a particular theme to the event? Think of the things you have in common that people can relate to. Everyone in the room has the location of the event and the food and beverages in common, so you can easily comment on those: "Great venue! Have you been here before? How did you hear about the event?" When you take sales out of the equation and focus on connecting, you take the pressure off yourself.

Think about common interests that have to do with news or your community. Has something funny happened recently in the national news, or is there something going on in your town that's newsworthy? Maybe there's a social media topic that's trending. If you're a sports buff or if a team in your city is doing well—like the Royals during the World Series and, thankfully, the Royals right now—mention that. Everyone in Kansas City also shares the experience of those darn construction cones from spring to fall. "Is there a lot of construction in your neighborhood right now? Is it causing a lot of traffic jams?" Conversation starters like that help break the ice because people can relate to the frustration.

Smalltalk can get old quickly, and at most networking events, you are there with a specific goal to accomplish. Asking simple questions can save you from awkward silences. You may not master the art of social jiujitsu immediately but will have numerous ways to break the ice. For example, if you were introduced to someone by your friend Steve, then start by asking, "How long have you known Steve?" Or try a variation on that theme: "How did the two of you meet?" It's also smart to ask, "What did Steve tell you about me?"

If you weren't introduced by anyone, then ask open-ended questions to get things rolling. Ask what that other person was hoping to get out of the event. Unless you know someone well, asking whether that person is connected to a particular person or company that would be a good connection for you is a little premature at this stage.

Introverts can also practice asking relatively easy and relatable questions. Here are a few more examples for those who're new to networking to try out:

- "Do you ever feel awkward when introducing yourself to someone you don't know? Yeah, me too."
- "What do you love or most enjoy about what you do?
- "What got you started in this business?
- "Have you been in the same career the entire time, or have you changed industries?"

...FIRE STARTERS

As conversation progresses, you might ask questions like: "Are there resources that would be helpful to you in your business? Do you volunteer anywhere, or are you associated with a non-profit? If so, are there any resources that would be beneficial for your organization?" Avoid questions that could be answered with a simple yes or no.

When you're at an event, one of the fastest ways to turn someone off is to keep the focus on you and monopolize the conversation. It's exhausting for them. Besides, the point of the networking event is connecting. Have you ever been in a conversation with someone and when you're done, you realized that they asked way more questions about you and it felt really good? You've met a fellow social jiujitsu master, and that's a valuable connection!

Once you've had a chance to see where the conversation and potential synergies are going, you can ask a question that was brilliantly crafted by networking guru Bob Burg: "How can I know if someone I'm speaking to is a good prospect for you?" His book *Endless Referrals* focuses on strategies like this to network your contacts into sales. If you're in sales or business development, this is an ideal question. If you'd like to put a slightly different spin on it, then ask, "How can I know if someone I'm speaking to is a good connection for you?" This expands the answer to include business or personal resources, strategic business connections, and more.

I'll stress that asking good questions is key to learning about other people and how you may be of assistance to them. Pay attention to their answers, and if they don't ask a single question about you, you may be on the receiving end of a hit-and-run.

HIT-AND-RUNS

Don't be the hit-and-run guy (or girl) at a networking event. You've met people like this, even if you don't know it. Everyone they meet gets a business card. As soon as they say, "Nice to meet you," they let you know how you can help them. Then they say, "We should get together for coffee," and they're off to their next targets. Definitely not a good impression!

Until you have time to get to know people and build a rapport with them, hold off asking for an introduction to anyone or any companies. If there's someone at the event you want to meet and you find someone who knows that person, briefly explain why you'd like that introduction. Think of a value you can add, not the sale you're looking to make. This isn't about sales. The point is to make a connection.

It can be easy to get caught up in a great conversation. Have a mental timer of approximately five minutes. At the five-minute mark of a conversation, pause and ask yourself if you're accomplishing your goal for being at the event. If there was a particular person you wanted to connect with then be sure you leave enough time to do that. If you're genuinely having a great conversation, then that's fantastic. Make sure that you trade contact information so you can continue the conversation later. You don't want to monopolize that person's time or have anyone monopolize yours.

If a conversation isn't going well and you need to escape, or if you don't see any common interests between you and the people you're talking to, then stop wasting your time and theirs. There are ways to leave a conversation politely. It's as simple as saying, "It was nice to meet, and I will leave you to connect with other people." Or you might say, "Excuse me. I need to use the restroom." Or say, "Excuse me. I need to make a call." You don't need to get anyone's card if you have no intention of following up with that person.

STELLAR ENTRANCES AND EXITS

If you see someone you want to meet but feel a little intimidated about walking up to the group of folks that person is standing with, the easiest thing to do is to ask the organizer for an introduction to the group. If you're flying solo, then pay attention to body-language cues. If there are two people talking and you don't know them, it's probably going to be harder to enter into that conversation, because unless one of them has that "I want to escape" look, they're most likely fully engaged in their conversation.

Typically, in groups of three, at least two of the three people will be engaged in the conversation, and there's an opportunity that you can approach the third person who seems less engaged. If people are facing directly towards each other, like three sides of a triangle—with their toes and shoulders all pointing inward toward each other—then they're fully engaged in the conversation. If they have a more open stance with their toes pointing out and shoulders open to the room, like two sides of a triangle, then that suggests they're more easily approachable. Also, look at their facial expressions. Do they have more serious expressions, or are they smiling and laughing?

I hear my mother's voice in my head, telling me to stand up straight and pull my shoulders back. It holds true not just for better posture but also for the confidence you project. If you slouch with your head down and your stomach out, you're saying to people that you are not sure of yourself. It's the small things that could be unconsciously turning people away without your being aware of it. It's important to pay attention to your body language, too. When you're talking to somebody and you fold your arms, even if it's unconsciously, that's sending signal that you're not approachable.

When people shift their posture from foot to foot and their eyes start wandering, then that means they're mentally checking out. You may have the same habits, so pay attention to yourself. A relaxed, open stance is inviting. When you're directly facing somebody, your shoulders and feet are pointing towards them and you're standing up straight. That's great posture.

Another important connecting advantage in conversation is to use a person's name when interacting with them. Dale Carnegie said, "A person's name is to him or her the sweetest and most important sound in any language." Using someone's name is a sign of courtesy, and and shows that you are paying attention. This small detail can make a positive and lasting impression.

And, as I mentioned in chapter four, maintain eye contact and resist the urge to look at the floor, as this shows you are paying attention to the people you're talking to and what they are saying. Eye contact, like handshakes, takes a little practice. Think Goldilocks and the three bears: too little could be interpreted as boredom, evasiveness, or even lack of confidence. Stare too much and too intently, and you may make the other person uncomfortable. Watch out for darting eyes, even in a busy environment. It's okay to glance down occasionally as long as you return your focus to the person quickly. Maintaining eye contact as you're saying goodbye will leave a positive impression.

And finally, don't forget to smile!

CARD COUNTERS

How do you get someone's business card at a networking event? The first rule of thumb is to be selective about whom you exchange information with. Your goal is *not* to collect as many business cards as you possibly can. Folks who do that are card counters. They're just at networking events for sport.

As your conversation develops with connections you make, there may be introductions you'd like to make or resources you can provide them with. Or you could simply want to keep track of where you met someone, a common interest you have, or the thing that stood out in your conversation. Jotting a quick note on the back of that person's card will help you to do a stellar job of following up later.

We've talked about body language and handshakes, but some cultures are much more strict about cards themselves as well as how they are presented at events or to individuals. Japan is one of those cultures. Make sure that you get permission before you start to write a note on someone's business card. If you're traveling or meeting with someone from another country, you may want to do some research on business card etiquette first.

Don't offer your card unless someone asks. You don't want to force your card on people because if they're not interested in what you have to say, you're wasting your time. It's kind of like getting junk mail at your house that you never asked for. Frankly, you're also wasting your cards. If you're interested in continuing the conversation, then ask for a card.

If you give your card to someone, that person may or may not contact you. Getting a card increases your chances of connecting, as long as you follow up.

You should always have business cards handy, so come prepared with plenty of cards and a pen because you never know when people whose information you want may have forgotten theirs. It's happened a couple of times that I've run out of cards at an event. You may have experienced some connecting karma like that, too. Those are the times when having technology can be a lifesaver. If you've had a great conversation and see the potential synergies, then consider connecting via social media. You'll need to determine the best platform, such as Twitter or Facebook. If you're a little bit more protective of your LinkedIn network, then you may not want to go there first.

#CONNECTINGHACK

CircleBack and CamCard are two business-card apps that capture an image of a business cards and create contacts in a user's phone.

AND A WINGMAN

A great way to maximize connections at an event is to take a wingman. I've mentioned it before, but be careful not to fall into your comfort zone and then only hang out with people you know all night. The whole point of having a wingman is to be making connections for each other. You have a couple of options for stretching your comfort zone. You can either walk together and make a very simple introduction for each other as you meet people. Or you can divide and conquer. This gives you a chance to multiply your one-on-one conversations.

Having or being a wingman is another example of how handy your RAS can be. Stay focused on what you're looking for. The person you're talking to may be an ideal introduction for your wingman compadre or vice versa. Either way, by making the introduction, you have created a serendipitous opportunity. And it's always great to open doors for people who you know deliver great results for their clients.

One example is Greta Perel. She's one of my go-to people for writing my clients' LinkedIn profiles. It's so easy to make introductions for her because she has done stellar work for me and is a terrific resource whom I can refer with the utmost confidence. Even though we live on the opposite sides of the city and don't compare calendars, we inevitably run into each other several times a month. Whether at an event or one-on-one meeting, LinkedIn has a tendency to come into the conversation. When Greta is close by, I always make the introduction.

Use your RAS to tune in when you go into an event because, as a connector, you have the ability to open lots of doors. Having a wingman takes the pressure off of you and, more importantly, it demonstrates the art of connecting to people you meet. Have you heard the saying, "We teach others how we want to be treated"? When you're connecting people, your behavior shows your mindset about making connections and how you manage relationships. You can also maximize your influence when people see that you're somebody who wants to be that interconnector for others. That's highly valuable.

ISLAND ALLIANCES

Having a wingman is great, and sometimes you may want to attend an event with a few folks who understand group collisions and can use their highly-tuned RAS to identify valuable connections to create a greater effect.

In her book *Families*, Jane Howard writes, "Call it a clan, call it a network, call it a tribe, call it a family. Whatever you call it, whoever you are, you need one." In this book, we'll refer to them as island alliances.

Who is an island alliance for you? Who are you having high-level conversations with on a regular basis, not just coffee chats? Island alliances are trusted compadres who focus on helping each other build their businesses and expand each other's networks. You've taken the time to really get to know them, and you know that they're a great fit for you on a number of levels. You align in a business sense and can easily open doors for each other, but these are also the folks you kick back with on a Friday night for happy hour and great conversation.

If you are stranded on a desert island, think about the people you would want to be stranded with. Who are the super-cool people you want to hang out with and know beyond doubt will have your back? You also know they're smart and great at what they do in their particular business. These are the folks who get win-win types of relationships. It's folks whom you think so highly of that you can easily make introductions for them and they for you.

Think about how you can make introductions for your island alliances. If, for example, they're the wingmen you take with you to events. These can also happen at coffee shop collisions just like with the "nine connections in two hours" morning. Having a personal experience with their companies can help you tell their stories. The experience could be that you hired them or even referred them to clients and have gotten the clients' positive feedback on their experiences. They may also be people you see as a valuable strategic alliances. Even if you don't have any experience with them, they might have been highly recommended by several other alliances who do.

In order to tell their stories well, you'll want to know more than just their 30-second commercials. Spend time getting to know them so you can learn about what makes them unique, the types of clients they best serve, the particular industries they focus on, what industries or clients do they *not* want to work with, the services they provide, the people who are their go-to strategic alliances, how they manage their business relationships, etc. There are alliances that may look like you are competitors on the surface but, when you dive into the details, you discover that you may be in the same industry but have different areas of expertise, or there are some industries you work with that they won't. This is another reason to take time to get to know someone beyond their LinkedIn profile. It will also help you to know who they are looking to meet and how best to introduce them to someone else.

THAT'S A WRAP

We've covered numerous events and other places you can go to make great connections. You know more now about what to do, what not to do, what to say, how to arrive, and how to leave, too. If you're feeling bold, then venture off on your own. Otherwise, grab a wingman or an island alliance. Just know all the effort has gone to waste if you fail on the follow-through. Never fear: we've outlined that process in chapter six!

ACTION

You're at the end of another chapter, so it's time to decide what you will take action on. And, be sure to schedule time to complete them sooner than later.

Fast Start

One-Hour Win

Snail It

CHAPTER 6

FOLLOWING UP, FALLING DOWN, AND MISSED CONNECTIONS

You made the connections you wanted, gathered a plethora of business cards, and now it's time to follow up. I don't want to be the bearer of bad news, but gathering all those business cards won't mean anything unless you follow up.

THE FORTUNE IS IN THE FOLLOW-UP

No one wants to bother folks who are valuable connections, especially after first meeting them. If you're procrastinating about—or "creatively avoiding"—contacting people after you've gotten their cards, you may have a mindset block. Maybe you're afraid of rejection or being seen as pushy.

I've seen surprising statistics about following up:

- Sirius Decisions, a leading B2B (business-to-business) research and advisory firm, found the average salesperson only attempts to reach potential clients twice.

- InsideSales.com's ResponseAudit™ research shows that 30 percent of prospects who contact businesses online never receive responses.

- Cardone Enterprises surveyed over 800 salespeople and 500 businesses and found three follow-up problems: having too many leads, letting leads go cold, and not having an organized follow-up process.

These are follow-up statistics for salespeople, whose paychecks depend on following up. Consider your own follow-up and follow-through statistics. After making an initial connection, why not spend five minutes to follow up? What's it costing you not to?

There's a fine line between being politely persistent and stalking. If you've reached out and haven't gotten a reply in a week, try changing it up. Don't send the same email at the same time of day on the same day of the week. I have seen statistics that say there are better times than others to send out emails or invitations on LinkedIn. But getting people to respond can sometimes just come down to catching them at the right time. If you've always followed up in the morning, try a different time of day. And if someone does ask you to stop following up, stop following up. But until then, you've got responsibility as a connector to keep trying.

Keep in mind that people who are well-connected can get a hundred emails a day. Depending on what they have on their schedules, it can be pretty tough to respond to every email. Some emails will naturally fall to the bottom of the priority list. If you don't get a response, it doesn't mean that someone is ignoring you. It just may mean that the person you're trying to follow-up with is too busy right then.

Following up also means you've got to be clear about what you're looking for in a connection. In Kansas City, we have something called "Midwest nice." It's something that drives me crazy. You meet somebody, have a great conversation, and then that person says, "Please, reach out to me any time." Then you follow up, but they seem to have gone into the witness protection program. *Don't* be that person. Being clear in your communication and in your intent reflects positively on you. If people in your city also have just one or two degrees of separation, then you could easily develop a reputation for being flaky or insincere.

If you've just met somebody, had a great conversation, and exchanged cards, it should mean that you're being invited to follow up. But don't take it personally if the other person goes into the witness protection program and completely vanishes. A lot of people do take it personally when they don't hear back from someone right away. Don't over-think it or craft your own story about why this person hasn't responded to you. Resist the urge to get upset or mad, and never take your feelings out on that person in an email. Maintain a polite tone in every email you send that person. Something you could say in a follow-up email is, "I know how busy you are. I completely understand if you just haven't had the time to respond, and I don't want to bombard you with emails if you're not interested. Whenever you have a moment, just let me know if you prefer I stop following up." That way, you'll be demonstrating that you're friendly and that you value that person's time, which is a good way to keep that person interested in you and avoid having someone be upset with you.

Ultimately, you're following up because you want to cultivate the connections you've made. If you're putting in the effort at events and one-on-one meetings, then do the same with following up. No matter whether you're in sales, a job transition, looking for potential clients, or seeking important information, following up matters. Remember, you teach people how to treat you, and your style of following up will demonstrate what you value in relationships. Be consistent with your follow-ups so that you stand out in a good way. You leave an impression after meeting someone, and your follow-up or lack thereof does, too.

237 BUSINESS CARDS

What can you do when you've gone to an event and gathered way too many cards? This section includes a few tips to help you prioritize and avoid being overwhelmed.

At the end of the day, spend a couple of minutes sorting through the cards that you've collected. Once you've sorted the cards, rank them in order of importance in terms of how each connection potentially fits into your network. Use the following categories to prioritize the cards:

1. Folks whom you see an immediate connection to and want to build strong relationships with. This category includes potential island alliances, great resource partners, or new clients.

2. The cool folks whom you don't immediately see a connection with, but you know they understand the importance of valuable relationships and can possibly open doors for you when it's appropriate, and you might be able to do the same for them.

3. Anyone whom you feel undecided about but haven't given up on yet.

Organizing and prioritizing the cards you've gathered will help you decide about how you should follow up. Start by contacting people whose cards you put in the first category. As you have time, reach out to the people in the second category and then to the people in the third category. If you wrote a reminder to yourself on the back of a card about why you wanted to reach out to that person, then make sure that information goes into your CRM for future reference. Was it a point of interest that you shared in common, or what was it that stood out about that person? Did you promise to send that person an article or even make a connection? It's critical that as you're following up you're getting the information stored in a safe place. Keeping a stack of business cards on your desk with a rubber band around them doesn't qualify and neither does an Excel spreadsheet, unless you've uploaded it to Dropbox or another web-based platform.

If you find yourself getting too behind on following up with regular one-on-one meetings, then consider scheduling fewer meetings a day so you can focus on following up with new connections. When it comes to conferences and the 237 or so cards you collected, well, that may take a little bit of extra work.

Following up in a timely manner gives you a major advantage over others in the business world. A good rule of thumb is to reach out to people within 24 to 48 hours of meeting them, up no matter which category they fell into. If you're attending a conference that runs multiple days, then the clock starts after the conference is over. On occasion, you may hit the three-day mark. That's really stretching it, but it's better to follow up than to let anyone forget you exist. Remember, we're not talking about diving in. We're talking about having a starting point for making great connections.

THE PERSONAL TOUCH

Now that you have your priorities in order, it's time to reach out. Having a simple follow-up strategy will save time and make you stand out in a sea of vanilla as a connector, not just someone who's networking.

Handwritten notes, in general, can be an effective part of your follow-up strategy. Consider which connections you want to cultivate strong relationships with, people who are in your first-priority category. Handwritten notes aren't necessary for everyone you meet, but sending a handwritten note to someone you're hoping to establish a strong relationship with after you've had a one-on-one meeting can add a human touch and help you stand out. If you wrote to everyone, you might start to feel like you're writing a novel. But for some connections, it might be worth your time.

You're fewer than six degrees from anyone you want to connect with, so discounting someone's value and not following up could come back to haunt you later. Staying connected by following up increases your collision rate. It feels good to get those notes, and it can feel just as good to spread cheer and congratulations to someone else. It's great when you meet someone who's already heard your name three times from other people whom you've followed up with. Even simple follow-up strategies can make a world of difference in future relationships.

In today's digital world, it can be a pleasant surprise to receive a phone call from people you've just met telling you how much they enjoyed the conversation you had. A voicemail has the same effect. Consider phone calls as part of your follow-up strategy and your relationship strategy in general. They don't have to take long, and it's a quick touch that can make someone's day.

Have you had the experience of thinking of someone who called you shortly thereafter? This happened to me recently, and it was great timing for everyone involved. The reason I say this is that it was a past client reaching out with an update about a project he had been working on for a couple of years. It was during the conversation I asked what resources he was looking for, and an international tax attorney and wealth advisor were at the top of his list. It just so happened that I had a meeting already scheduled with one of my island alliances who would be an ideal introduction. Considering the time I'd spent working with this client, I knew his business well and have even signed NDA's for my work with him, so I was privy to confidential information. In the past, I had facilitated introductions on his behalf, so it was an easy ask to invite him to the already-scheduled meeting. I then called my island alliance to let him know that the upcoming conversation was taking a slight detour and to give him a few background details about my client. I also took the opportunity to ask about another project of my own that my island alliance is advising me on. That simple phone call gave me a chance to catch up with my client, facilitate an introduction, and gain knowledge for myself all at the same time.

I love technology, but I also keep a planner to write down my goals, daily to-do's, ideas, and notes from meetings. I also jot down names of the people I want to touch base with via phone. Client conversations are at the top of the list. I also include island alliances and people I want to take a moment to follow up with from recent events or even past events. If there's a minute of downtime between meetings or at lunch, I'll make a quick call. It's ideal to talk with people live, but even quick messages can let them know you're thinking of them.

#CONNECTINGHACK

We mentioned Crystal—a fantastic service for crafting empathetic communication—in chapter one. Crystal can also help you research (not stalk) your new connections by using the 'view personality' function. Once installed, you'll find this button on LinkedIn and Facebook profiles as well as in the email plugin. The information gained can help you follow up more effectively.

Want to know if your follow-up email was read? If you use Gmail or Outlook for email, you can use Sidekick, Bananatag Email Tracking, or Intelliverse Email Tracker to find out when your email was opened. (If you use Chrome as your browser, you can also install plugins for these programs.) Some of these programs also show you how many times an email was opened, where the person was when the email was opened, and on what device they opened the email. All three offer a limited number of emails that can be tracked for free.

CASUALLY CONNECTING

Another way you can continue the follow-up process is via social media platforms. Look up any new connections who mentioned that they use social media to see which platforms they're on and what they're posting. No matter how well the conversation went, do a quick check before connecting. As entrepreneur and motivational speaker Jim Rohn once said, "You're the average of the five people you spend the most time with." Better to check the person out than regret making the connection.

Card counters can also be found on social media platforms. These are the folks whose sole intent is to connect to as many people as possible.

They will fish through your contacts to see who they can call. If they use your name as the connecting point, it doesn't reflect well on you if there's a bad experience. They may also be connected to people whom you don't want any affiliation with. I have people reaching out to connect to me constantly on all platforms. If they use foul language or post photos that I view as offensive, the last thing I want to do is to connect them to my network even if it's loosely. Facebook and Twitter are platforms where you see a wide variety of content, but it's less common to get questionable requests on LinkedIn. However, you'll still have people attempting to pilfer contacts.

Connecting to someone you've actually met and like is an easy decision. It's the ones you don't know whom you need to spend a little time reviewing before reaching out or accepting a connection.

Twitter provides a platform for a more casual connection. You can follow people, and they don't necessarily have to follow you back. If they don't, that speaks volumes in itself. But don't take it personally if they don't follow you in return. Maybe they don't use Twitter very often, or they may have discounted the potential collisions that can happen there.

Facebook was originally designed for connecting with friends, but the addition of business pages have expanded its reach. If you use it for family and friends only, Facebook may not be a platform you use often for following up with business connections, unless that connection turns into an island alliance. That said, I've made stellar connections on Facebook and even have clients whom I have connected with on Facebook once I've gotten to know them in person.

As mentioned in chapter four, your privacy settings will determine if people can actually find you and connect with you and vice versa. If you're using Facebook and Twitter for business, then adjust your settings accordingly.

I treat my LinkedIn connections differently than Facebook and Twitter connections. LinkedIn is about business. When I first started using

LinkedIn, I was all about connecting to anyone and everyone, no matter who it was. But as I gained more connections, it was difficult to manage the business relationships I was tracking there.

Take a quick tour through your existing LinkedIn contacts. If your memory is fuzzy about how you met or when you last saw someone you're connected to, or if you notice profiles with no profile photo and little background information, then you need to filter through those connections and possibly delete them.

If you want to connect with someone on LinkedIn, do not—I repeat, do not—send a standard invitation. You need to customize your invitations so that you stand out from the people who send just the automatic invitation that reads, "I'd like to connect on LinkedIn." Don't send an invitation when you're on smartphone, iPad, or tablet. Make sure that you're at a computer so you can customize your invitations.

Here are a few examples of customized invitations for folks you know and those you don't, replies to invitations you receive from people you don't know, and thank-you's, too. If you have that person's email address, then take a minute to draft an email with Crystal first, then determine the best greeting and signature. Tweak accordingly.

Invitation to someone you know

Hi [name],

Hoping today finds you doing well. Considering the number of mutual connections we share, I'm surprised we haven't connected on LinkedIn yet. Let's expand our networks.

Cheers!

[your name]

Invitation to someone you want to connect with but don't know

Hi [name],

I am always interested in connecting with likeminded professionals. After looking at your profile, I think you would be a great connection.

Please feel free to send me an invitation to connect. The email address I use for LinkedIn is [insert email address here]. Here is my direct link to connect: [your LI profile URL]. Also, I do realize you may be reading this from your mobile phone, so if it's easier, please send me your email address instead.

All the best,

[your name]

Response to someone you don't know who sends an invitation to connect

This response will weed out the folks who are just looking for numbers and not quality connections. Hit "Reply" in the invitation email you receive to send this message to the sender directly, without going through LinkedIn.

Hello [name],

Thank you for the invitation to connect. I use LinkedIn a little differently and am curious to know how you feel we could be of mutual benefit to each other. If there's someone I saw in your network whom I'd like to connect to, how might you make an introduction if I were to ask for one? Thanks again for the invitation, and I look forward to hearing from you.

Best,

[your name]

Invitation to someone who has viewed your profile but not sent you an invitation

Review the profile first to make sure it's someone you'd like to connect to.

Hello [name],

I noticed that you reviewed my profile. Thank you for stopping by. Connecting on LinkedIn with likeminded professionals is something that I value. It would be an honor to have you as a connection, and I hope you'll accept my invitation.

Best,

[your name]

Casual thank-you

Hi [name],

Thanks so much for connecting. Please let me know if there is anything I can help you with.

Enjoy the rest of your week!

[your name]

Formal thank-you

Dear [name],

Thank you for the invitation to connect. It's an honor to be included in your circle of influence. Please don't hesitate to reach out if I can be of assistance in your endeavors.

Best,

[your name]

#CONNECTINGHACK

It feels good to get those notes, and it can feel just as good to spread cheer and congratulations to someone else. Sending a handwritten note can be much more memorable than a casual social media message. But if you need to send a note quickly, you might consider sending a greeting online using an ecard or even a video. Eyejot is a great hack for that. It lets you create and send video messages like you would email. It may not take the place of a handwritten note, but it's more personal than the average inbox message. That added personal touch will help you stand out and strengthen your connection.

If you think that sending a handwritten note might take too much time, or you don't have any good stationery at hand, try Hello Bond, which sends handwritten notes on your behalf. A potential client who gets a handwritten note from you out of the blue will certainly find you more memorable. After all, how often does anyone get a handwritten note anymore?

A warning, especially for millennials: I know that a lot of you rely heavily on texting for daily communication, but don't use texting for following up on a potential connection. Connecting requires a human touch. The #connectinghacks I mention throughout the book highlight technology that can help you be more human, empathetic, and personal in your communication. But sometimes—especially when you're first establishing a connection—it's better to take the technology out of the equation and reach out the old-fashioned way with a phone call or a handwritten note. That may be out of your comfort zone for connecting, but making those direct connections to people on a personal level is something that's going to elevate you above the rest.

There are many ways that you can keep from getting lost in the vanilla sea, so be creative. Set yourself apart, because when you do, you'll be laying the foundation for making the extraordinary professional relationships that are essential to your career.

FALLING DOWN

Falling down is also known as follow-up fails, and there are some common follow-up fails you need to avoid. One of the worst follow-up mistakes that I see people make is to put people on an email list after meeting them for the first time. It happens all the time. I meet somebody at an event, and the next thing I know, I've ended up on a marketing email list even though I barely know the person and didn't give permission or express any interest in being put on an email list. That, to me, is completely rude and a total connecting fail. Unless people specifically say, "Yes, I want to get your marketing information," don't send them spam!

People can easily get inundated with emails from all the lists they've signed up for, let alone the ones they *didn't* ask to be signed up for. When speaking at a conference, I always have a sign-up sheet in the back of the room, which people use to share their contact information. The sign-up sheet also has information about my app, which they can download immediately to stay current about what I'm doing with trainings, new products, and events. This gives people a choice about how they want to connect with me and receive updates.

A similar follow-up fail happens with spam on social media platforms. Someone sends you a friend request or an invitation to connect. You check the person out, and it seems like he or she would be a good person to connect to. So you accept the invitation. The next thing you know, you're getting bombarded with marketing messages like "Try this new product!" or "There's something I really want to share with you." I've seen this more than a few times on Facebook and even on LinkedIn. To me, it's one of the worst follow-up fails. It shows that you're a novice, that you don't get relationships, and that what you care about is selling someone, not making a connection.

Recently, I connected with a gentleman at an event who later friended me on Facebook. From what I gathered during our conversation and feedback from a mutual connection, it certainly looked like there was some value to making this connection. But then he sent me a message on Facebook that said, "Can I have your email?" Had he done his research, he would have found that my email was in my "About" section. I sent him my email address and thought that meant I should expect an email from him to continue the conversation he seemed to want to start. Instead, I ended up on a massive list of people—whom he did not blind carbon copy—about an event that he was promoting.

Don't be that person. When you meet people at an event, you want to get to know them and inquire about their interests so that you can make valuable connections. Then follow up with a phone call or a note as soon as you can. This isn't about you. This is about making great connections. So do not be that person. Get permission and do it right when you're reaching out to cultivate connections.

#CONNECTINGHACK

Depending on how important you think a new relationship is going to be, you may want to use a CRM to help you be strategic about following up.

We covered Nimble—the CRM that makes profiles on your contacts based on your notes and on their updates on social media platforms—in chapter two. Nimble is a great hack if you're focusing on the art of social selling. For business development, Contactually is a great hack because you can use it to schedule emails, track client recommendations and conversions, and organize projects you're working on for clients. Insightly, Zoho, and HubSpot are also great CRM options.

You can find a more complete list of #connectinghacks at my

www.yourconnectingadvantage.com/connectinghacks

Make sure that you're using the right follow-up system because, frankly, an Excel spreadsheet is not going to cut it, especially if you're looking at being a connector. Nor will a stack of business cards sitting on your desk with notes on the back. You need to find a way that you can clearly manage client information and follow-ups. So take some time and figure out what's going to be best for you.

TOP-OF-MIND OR BOTTOM OF THE BARREL

Now that you've done your initial follow-up, you'll also want to be thinking about how you can stay top-of-mind with new connections.

For example, when you're reaching out to potential clients to ask if they've come to a decision about moving forward with a project, think about how you can be sending or offering value that helps you stand out. I always try to add value whenever possible, even if it's just an extra bit of information—a link to an interesting article or news item—within an email. Sometimes, I'll reach out to someone out of the blue just to say, "I was thinking of you." These are ways that you can use a human touch to help you stand out.

You can also use LinkedIn's message tool to stay top-of-mind with the people who are of top importance to you and to whom you want to add value regularly. The intent isn't to spam anyone but to send an article you think they might find of interest. Note that the option to send a group message without allowing recipients to see each other's names and email addresses is no longer available with the new LinkedIn message center rollout. Because of this change, I'd suggest only sending a group message when you're introducing your connections to each other or else it could be perceived as spam.

If you are already connected with someone who you think will be a valuable connection (like a potential client or strategic resource), then keep a folder with articles or videos that may be of interest to that person. Some online resources for keeping connection folders include Google Drive, Dropbox, and OneDrive. You can also create bookmarks in a browser for later reference. You can share the content you save in the folder with that person sometime in the future, either when you are connected via social media or through email.

As I mentioned in chapter two, you can use social media to make more personal connections. Facebook and LinkedIn will give you notifications about special occasions—like birthdays, work anniversaries, promotions, and participation in events or trainings—for most people, depending on how they've configured their privacy settings. Invitations to future events give you another option for staying top-of-mind. Reach out to the contacts whom you've really connected with to see if they will be at the same event where you met. This gives you a chance to reconnect before and at the event.

You can also ask those contacts if they want to be kept the in the loop about future events that you think they might be interested in. Here's where the fun happens. Consider inviting a couple of people to an event that you'll be at. If they don't already know each other, you've just expanded their worlds. The bonus is that you're already attending the event, so you're going to get the benefit of making a connection with a minimal time investment. There's the potential of a "nine connections in two hours" moment because you can expand the base of relationships for multiple people at one event by introducing them to a lot of great people. Remember to test the waters first, because the last thing you want is to invite an "all hat and no cattle" person who really doesn't understand connecting at all!

MISSED CONNECTIONS

Details matter when it comes to having a successful follow-up. Recently, I had two almost-missed connections in the same week. I left messages for two folks whom I know fairly well. One was interested in attending a workshop. When I called, there was no personalized voicemail greeting, so I didn't know if I'd actually gotten her voicemail or someone else's voicemail. I left a message because I was under a time crunch and needed to get the phone call off my to-do list. That was on Monday. After not getting a response all week, I ran into her at an event on Friday. When I spoke to her there, she said, "Yeah, I've got you on my list of people to call. I've just been super-busy." She didn't realize that her voicemail greeting is canned. It's details like these that matter, though, because she's launching a new business. What if I were a potential client calling?

The second connection that was a near-miss was with an individual who had started working in sales at a new company, so even though the phone number I called still had her personalized voicemail greeting, voicemail messages weren't getting to her because she was no longer employed at that company. This is the reason to work through the 'other final four' steps in chapter one. If you have switched companies, you've switched phone numbers and email addresses, so you need to make that people know your new information. There could be an opportunity you missed because you didn't follow up and let people know.

FOLLOWING VILFREDO

At the beginning of the chapter, I mentioned those less-than-stellar follow-up statistics. But there's a way to be strategic about your follow-ups using the Pareto principle. The Pareto principle—in case you're not familiar with it—asserts that there's an 80 percent to 20 percent ratio for almost anything, such as causes and results. In any given situation, 80 percent of the results are determined by 20 percent of the causes.

In business, the 80/20 rule, as the Pareto principle is sometimes called, is often used as a guideline for following up with sales. The idea is that 80 percent of your sales will come from 20 percent of your customers. It also applies to cultivating relationships. The key is to focus most of your energy on activities that produce the best outcomes for you. Hence, the reason for a connecting strategy. Follow-up and follow-through are critical to your connecting success. This is why 20 percent of the people get 80 percent of the results. Be *that* guy!

ACTION

Now it's time to follow up with yourself about the top things you are taking action on. Write them down, make them happen, and give yourself kudos for accomplishing them.

Fast Start

One-Hour Win

Snail It

CHAPTER 7

SUPER-CONNECTORS, ESSENTIAL INFLUENCERS, AND COOL KIDS

You may have heard of super-connectors before, and you probably know one. Keith Ferrazzi, author of *Never Eat Alone*, gives the following definition for a super-connector: "Super-connectors are people who maintain contact with thousands of people in many different worlds and know them well enough to give them a call. Restauranteurs, headhunters, lobbyists, fundraisers, public relations people, politicians, and journalists are the best super-connectors because it's their job to know *everyone*."

SUPER-CONNECTORS

Do you know any super-connectors? They could be people you work with or know through business circles. Or maybe you've run into them on the soccer field or at your place of worship. Not only do they seem to know everyone, they have influence and are great at making solid introductions.

That super-connector could also be you.

The term *super-connector* is not to be used for just anyone who seems be well-connected. Super-connectors have a few defining characteristics:

- An intuitive understanding about who needs to know whom, even though there isn't an obvious reason for the connection.
- A desire to expand their own networks by including others instead of limiting their networks by judging or dismissing

others based on their jobs, geographic locations, where they work, etc.

- A willingness to share their insider knowledge with you once you're in their circles of trust (more on that later in this chapter).

- A reputation for being cool people to hang out with, because they believe success doesn't happen without significance or the desire to achieve something greater, like through philanthropic work or by leaving behind a legacy of being a difference-maker.

If you think you can't be a connector, let alone a super-connector, reconsider that mindset. When I say this to people, I often hear them respond with, "I just wasn't born with that gift" or "But I'm not an extrovert." Good news! Connecting isn't a natural ability that some people are just born with. No matter whether you're an introvert or extrovert, and no matter what your age, career, and geographic location are, you have the ability to become a connector when you apply a connecting strategy, are willing to push your comfort zones, and shift what you think is possible.

WHAT'S YOUR NUMBER?

The power of super-connectors isn't only based on how many connections they have. You might have the impression that they're just one or two—not six—degrees of separation from everyone. Their power as connectors is also related to the Dunbar number.

Maybe you've heard that most of us have an average of 100 to 250 people in our *networks*—our closest, most stable, and most influential connections. That average is known as the Dunbar number, named after anthropologist Robin Dunbar. The idea behind the Dunbar number is that it takes brain power to maintain close social relationships. And you have limited room to store information about each person who's in your network and their relationships to one another. That's part of the reason that larger circles of social relationships can be unstable. A network will be more stable if its boundaries are based on clear purposes and values.

Social media can dramatically increase social capital and breadth of your network. Do the math: if you have 500 direct connections on LinkedIn and they each have 150 of their own connections that might be valuable for you, that's 75,000 potential connections. When you include third- and fourth-degree connections, the number of potential connections exponentially explodes!

Ask yourself how many people you're connected to on Facebook. How many of those people do you actually know? Which groups are you a part of on Facebook? How often do you interact? And then add Instagram, YouTube, Google+, about.me, Pinterest, and any other social media platforms you're active on. How many people subscribe to your email list, if you've got one?. Are you keeping them engaged with regular communication? A passive list of contacts doesn't amount to anything. Sending an article or newsletter once a year isn't going to do a lot. Expecting people just to find your blog or website on their own produces the same meager results. If you're staying active on the sites you use and keeping your followers engaged, you're increasing your collision rate and making the most of your potential connections.

Super-connectors aren't just looking at the numbers game, though. They understand that, like with crops, cultivating connections takes time and work. They realize the importance of planting, nurturing, and then harvesting. They know influence isn't about size of their networks but about the quality, stability, and value of relationships.

They don't think, "He who dies with the most contacts in his Rolodex wins" (does anyone even use those anymore?). If you want to be a super-connector, you'll need to focus on making connections on a deeper level, taking time regularly to nurture relationships and consistently engage others to create meaningful interactions.

VALUE-ADDS AND VIRAL COMMENTS

Adding value to super-connectors through online platforms can be done several ways. If you are building your influence by blogging, then you can mention a super-connector who's relevant to the topic in a post and link directly to that person's website or LinkedIn profile. You can also mention that person in a podcast about that topic or in a Google Hangouts series that you host. Sharing your podcast or Hangouts series on your website and social media platforms will add value because you're exposing a broader audience of your followers to that person by posting content that you've made permanently available online.

Twitter gives you an easier way to add value to super-connectors by using mentions and retweets. Start with your tweet, then tag the person whom you want to reach out to. Make sure that your tweet has content that is relevant or interesting to that person, not spam. You could also retweet one of that super-connector's tweets. The super-connector will then get a notification that you've shared a tweet with your followers.

Facebook provides you with similar ways to add value to super-connectors. You can mention people and business pages in posts you make to your personal profile and to your business's page by typing the name of the person or business that you want to tag in the text of your post. You can also share super-connector's posts with your friends—if you're posting from your personal profile—or with your business page's followers. Remember, if you're sharing a post from someone's personal profile, that person's privacy settings may limit which of your friends and followers can see the post. And don't spam that person's profile or business page with lots of posts from either your personal profile or your business's page.

LinkedIn also gives you the ability to share posts from other super-connectors and subject-matter experts you're following. With such a wide variety of well-connected and influential folks to follow on LinkedIn, you'll have an abundance of opportunities to share content from people you're hoping to build connections to. Craft a few sentences when you share their content, and if you're directly linked to them, then mention their names in the post from them as well.

If you're posting content from someone who is also on Twitter, consider this strategy to get a little more bang for your buck. It's an extra step that takes a minute or two, but it's definitely worth it. Using the same share button, post the content you're sharing only to Twitter. What you'll find is if that individual is on Twitter as well as LinkedIn, the post will have that person's Twitter handle with "@" in the post. On occasion, I find that someone is on Twitter but hasn't included a Twitter handle, so it takes an additional step for a quick search on that platform to find that handle and make the post. Depending on the content, I will tweak the post slightly to personalize the tweet.

Here are a couple of sample posts, to give you a few ideas about how to write these cross-platform posts in LinkedIn:

Automatic post via LinkedIn to Twitter

"How to Master the Art of Social Selling" by @jeff_haden on @ LinkedIn www.LinkedIn.com/pulse/how-master-latest-sales-strategy-social-selling-jeff-haden

Slightly tweaked post with a subject hashtag—the "#" symbol—and Jeff's name mentioned at the beginning

#SocialSelling insight from @jeff_haden "How to Master the Art of Social Selling" via @LinkedIn www.LinkedIn.com/pulse/how-master-latest-sales-strategy-social-selling-jeff-haden

If the people whom you want to mention aren't already in any of your Twitter lists, then be sure and add them to a list so that you can easily see the content they are posting in their feeds as well as who else is mentioning them in tweets. This makes retweeting content that's of interest to super-connectors a breeze.

YOUR SUPER CONNECTION LIST

Clarify your strategy for connecting with super-connectors by writing down the names and companies of the people whom you want to reach out to. Making a list will engage your RAS. These relationships will take time to cultivate, so prioritize your list. The goal isn't to write down as many names as you can but to determine a few specific people whom you want to explore relationships with. Send this list out to those in your network who may be able to help you connect to the people on your list. Circulate the names via email or through phone calls to people in your network. If you don't tell people in your network about whom you want to meet, you could be missing opportunities and making it harder to connect.

Research where those super-connectors spend their time online. Are there any platforms that you use—blogs, podcasts, Hangouts, social media, etc.—that that they also use? If you don't use many of the same platforms, consider other options. Research who's in their network and find out what mutual connections you already have. Check multiple social media platforms to make sure you've identified all possible mutual connections. Stay focused on your connecting strategy so that you don't get too scattered trying to connect with just anyone on platforms you don't really use. Remember, this isn't stalking; it's research, so it's ok to be thorough.

Watch your self-talk when you're reaching out to super-connectors because it's easy to talk yourself out of making a connection. If you don't ask, the answer will always be no. Even though some of these connections might seem impossible to make, you're going to find that it takes much less time to make serendipitous collisions once you get connected to other connectors.

THEY SAID YES!

Have you ever missed an amazing opportunity because you were afraid to make the ask? It could simply be for assistance or help. When you're focused on connecting with or on becoming a super-connector, there's always a chance that you may be ignored or—even worse—rejected. Who wants to be rejected? I bet you have encountered the type of person who doesn't give up whether in business or in their social lives. They make their move, and if they get rejected, they bounce back with a better opening line and determination to make their presence known again. These are super-connectors.

I learned many years ago that if you don't ask, the answer is always no. You never know what the outcome will be, so you might as well ask. When the Kansas City Royals got to the World Series in 2014, I made a post on my Facebook page in the hopes of snagging a ticket: "To the wonderful person who's taking me to the World Series - I'm available for ANY game in KC (or even 2). I'll be happy to pay for parking, food and beverages. Just let me know when I need to be ready!!"

I got a total of 59 likes and 17 comments on that post, including: "Good try Layman, hope it works," "Have a good time as I know you WILL be there," "Yes, asking is the key. So many don't," and "www.andwhosaysJoyceLaymanisnotcharming.com."

The result of the ask was that I got to attend Game 6, the incredible 10-0 blowout. Our seats were on the front row, overlooking the Giants' bullpen. The tickets were $750 each, but this experience of a lifetime only cost me $25 for parking. When I asked the person who invited me about why he took me to the game, his reply was, "I wanted you to have your yes."

Am I afraid of being rejected? Of course! Have you met anyone who actually likes rejection? It's one of the fears that stops us from going after what we really want.

Karen Harrison—founder of Joy of Living—is the owner of a company that provides pet sitting, dog walking, and pet taxi services. As an animal advocate, Karen launched *Fully Feline*, an online magazine. We happened to be at a Central Exchange event together to hear *New York Times* bestselling author Bradley Trevor Grieve talk about his book *Why Dogs are Better Than Cats*. Karen took "If you don't ask, the answer is always no" to heart and asked Bradley for a feature interview on her blog. Because of his bestselling author status, his publisher, Andrews McMeel, got involved. The request was granted, and interview was published. Karen used that yes to make additional asks of other pet gurus, which in turn added additional value for her clients and readers.

If you find yourself creatively avoiding asking for an introduction to a super-connector, it's time to stretch your comfort zone. To get a different outcome, you need to change your approach. I mentioned LB's and NT's in *Just Another Leap*. These are what I call "liked best" and "next time." Ask yourself, "What did I like best about how I made the ask? Did it go well?" If you don't think so, then what would you do differently if given a chance for a do-over?" Learn from what you perceive as a connecting fail—because it may not be—and consider what you can do differently next time to get the outcome you're looking for.

An easy way to do this is think back to a time when you reached out with what you thought was an impossible ask but got a yes in response. Relive the scene in your mind using the visualization techniques mentioned in chapter three. Think about what you said, what you did, and—most importantly—how you felt. Use this as your springboard for having a different mindset for the next connecting opportunity.

ESSENTIAL INFLUENCERS

Dale Carnegie published How to Win Friends and Influence People in 1937, and the premise of his book is as true now as it was then: improving on one's interpersonal skills is mandatory for every super-connector. Carnegie's research showed that people who have superior social skills are substantially more influential than people with average social skills. Their power is based in part on the amount of social capital that they develop in building relationships with the people in their networks. That social capital is built by more than just "friending" people on Facebook or sending and accepting invitations to connect on LinkedIn. It has to do with the power that super-connectors—the folks who've been working hard at building up that social capital—can have in any given situation. Super-connectors who use their social capital to help the people they're connected to achieve their goals are known as influencers. Close friends, island alliances and even your clients and super-connectors can be influencers.

No matter whether you're in a leadership position within your organization, solopreneur, or head of the PTA and can make things happen—like opening up an opportunity to the right person for the right reason—then you have influence. If you know powerful people and can reach them when you need to, that's influence. If people see you as an expert in a particular area or as a strategic thinker for making creative solutions or for finding someone who can, that makes you influential.

Influencers care about more than just business because they understand that influence is directly related to the strength of relationships. Influence increases when you develop meaningful relationships by taking the time to get to know someone and to develop mutual trust and respect. Influence is also related to value. When people know how much they gain from having you in their networks, they're thinking about the level of influence you have. It also speaks directly to your presence, that feeling someone gets from being with you and from the impression you leave behind. Influence isn't necessarily a position or a title; it's based on relationships with others.

If there's someone whom you want to meet and are asking another person to make an introduction for you, be sure to find out whether that person has influence with the person you want to meet and is willing to use it on your behalf. Too often, people think that because they know one person within a group or an organization they can easily get access to the group's key leaders. That's not always the case, especially in larger companies.

In the "six degrees of Kevin Bacon" exercises that I facilitate for conference attendees, sales teams, clients, etc., it's easy to turn six degrees of separation into one or two. The hurdle is discovering who the right person is, the person who has influence with whoever someone else wants to meet and is willing to make that introduction. The higher up the food chain you go in a company, the more you're asking of the person who's making that introduction for you. Your influencer has to be sure that whoever you want to be introduced to does a little research on you, they'll see that you're a valuable connection. No matter whether you're the influencer who's making an introduction or you're asking others to use their influence to make introductions for you, be sure to hold up your end of the deal. When an influencer makes a connection on your behalf, you can be rest assured you won't be getting crickets on the other end of the phone.

When it comes to getting things done, influencers use their networks to give advice and shape the behavior of their connections. In *The Influentials*, Ed Keller and Jonathan Berry write that 10 percent of people who are engaged in their communities are recognized as being sources of reliable advice and give advice five times more than the average person. Keller's research also indicates that when folks get word-of-mouth product recommendations, two-thirds of them are motivated to buy the products that were recommended or something similar.

For those of you questioning the tiny size of your networks and wondering whether it's possible to have influence, the answer is yes. But it may not happen overnight. This is why it's important to be strategic and to be open to connections. If you want to be an influencer, it's critical that your personal brand make the best impression it can on others. If people don't know you or can't find information on you in a Google search, then you are going to have a difficult time influencing them or demonstrating your own influence. One person can open up a world of possibilities to you if it's the right person.

POWER DYNAMICS

You might be looking to connect with that one influential person, and you might think you've got a lot to offer that person, but mega-influencers won't know what you've got to offer until you can show them. Consider the power dynamics of the situation. I would love it if *Shark Tank*'s Barbara Corcoran wanted to hang out with me. But I would need to give her a good reason to get together, since there are lots of people who'd want to be in her network of connections. This is why being clear about your value is important. You have to know how you can help the people whom you want to connect to and be able to communicate your value to them.

Even the most successful people had to start somewhere with their networks. It's the uber-successful folks who continue to keep themselves open to connections whom I most admire. They don't prejudge anyone who's coming up in the ranks because they know all connections have the potential to be powerful. In their tanks, even a small fish can turn into a whale.

When I reached out to Bob Burg with the simple request for a comment on a talk that I was giving, I had no idea that we would develop a strong connection. He was certainly out of my league when it came to my network at the time. I immediately shifted to having the mindset of a go-giver!

AND I'D LIKE TO INTRODUCE YOU TO...

Sometimes, you can use simple things and coincidences to demonstrate your value. That's what happened when the contact I made through an online dating site introduced me to the CEO of a successful startup. When I looked up the CEO on LinkedIn, I discovered that the two of them weren't connected, even though they'd known each other for years. By pointing this out to them, I gave them a small but useful opportunity to create connections across their linked professional networks that might otherwise have been missed.

Introductions are one key asset that you can offer to anyone who's invested in connections. Consider what kinds of introductions you can offer and how they could be helpful. You might know a potential client or someone who could expand a network for someone else. Recently, I made an introduction between the head of a bank and a high-net-worth financial advisor. Both are great people who work with similar types of clients who understand relationships and would make easy island alliances for each other. The preliminary introduction was made via email, with links to their LinkedIn profiles included so that they could do their research to make the meeting more productive. I facilitated the conversation over lunch. We found out that they also have another mutual connection in common who hadn't introduced them. I had directed a workshop that the mutual connection and financial advisor had recently attended, and it turns out that he's also the banker's best friend. I'm always looking to help make connections like these because the one or two degrees of separation between people in Kansas City doesn't always connect. I'm always looking to make connections that others might miss, and I've learned not to take connections for granted. Great people need to know each other!

Remember not to make a snap judgment about people who offer to make introductions for you until you know something about them.

You never know who they know and the type of influence they have in their networks. Turning down their offers to make introductions could potentially cost you the connection and their motivation to make another introduction.

PERFECTLY PLANNED COLLISIONS

A great way to expand your influence is by coordinating organized gatherings. Perfectly planned collisions give you opportunities to create serendipitous moments for others. An easy way to do this is simply to invite a guest to attend an event with you. The great thing about this is that you don't have to put the effort in to coordinate the event, but you can capitalize on the connections who you know will be there. You can show value to multiple people by introducing them to each other, yet all you've done is shown up and possibly pay the small entrance fee.

In the next sections, we'll go over some additional ways that you can create perfectly planned collisions and establish yourself as an influencer.

Highly Focused Happy Hours

To borrow the words of Jimmy Buffet, "It's 5 o'clock somewhere," and that means it's time for happy hour, so why not make it strategic? You don't necessarily have to plan a happy hour by yourself. You can partner with others to do this. Ideally, you'd partner with one or more of your island alliances. You know each other well, have great synergies, and have connections who need to know each other. When you bring the right people together at a happy hour, synergies happen. The key is for you to be facilitating the connections that take place while there. I've co-hosted several strategic happy hour events with my island alliances. We were very strategic about whom we invited. There was a vetting process to determine how we felt each attendee could add value to the other attendees. Most importantly, they had influence and had shown their willingness to use it on our behalves or on the behalf of someone whom we introduced them to.

The invitation to the happy hour was very clear regarding the purpose of the event, which was strictly to expand meaningful relationships. No sales allowed! Each of the alliances who were organizing the happy hour contacted individuals to invite them and then followed up with invitations. Once the attendee list was confirmed, we sent the entire list—with contact information included—to everyone who was invited so that they could see who else would be in the room and have time to do their research. We asked attendees to let us know whom they wanted an introduction to at the happy hour. The goal was to help them make three to five great connections, so camping at tables was discouraged. Like clockwork, we would make an introduction and leave them to have a conversation. Five to ten minutes later, we would check to see how things were going and whisk that our guests off to their next introductions. Once the event was over, we sent follow-up communications with the final attendee list to ensure everyone had each other's contact information. If someone no-showed, they weren't invited back. In their feedback, people said that the happy hour was unlike any networking event that they'd ever been to. An introduction at one of our happy hours even resulted in the sale of a four-million-dollar company. When you put great people in a room together, cool things happen!

Mastermind Dinners

In the process of writing *Your Connecting Advantage*, I was fortunate to learn about mastermind dinners. Hosting strategic happy hours has been fantastic, but after learning about the connections Jayson Gaignard created with his dinners, hosting a mastermind dinner is next on my agenda!

Jayson is an entrepreneur, author of *Mastermind Dinners*, and the founder of the top-rated MastermindTalks podcast. This qualifies him as a super-connector. His story is full of ups, downs, and stellar rebounds. His company Ticket Canada was doing $5 million a year in sales. Thanks to his business partner, he went from flying high to $250,000 in personal debt in just over a month. In an interview with *Entrepreneur*, Jayson said, "When you hit rock bottom, you'll be left with two things: the integrity of your word and your relationships. Never tarnish your word and always invest in your network."

In the midst of chaos, Jayson saw an opportunity and went all-in on creating his now-famous Mastermind Dinners. If I told you the whole story, then you won't feel prompted to read his book, but you should. In a nutshell, his dinners are designed around intimate groups of four to six people. Just like we carefully planned our happy hours, Jayson spends hours on planning the guest list, picking the right location, and developing strategies for keeping the conversation going. Even when he was struggling financially, he still picked up the entire bill for the dinners. His goal was to deliver a once-in-a-lifetime experience for all involved and to provide an environment for meaningful conversations and authentic connections. The dinners have now evolved into Mastermind Talks. Jayson has hosted the who's-who of entrepreneurs, including the creator of Bulletproof Coffee, Dave Asprey; hedge fund manager James Altucher; Aubrey Marcus, the founder of Onnit; and Tim Ferris, bestselling author of *The 4-Hour Workweek.*

Jayson put his success formula into his book, *Mastermind Dinners.* It's the step-by-step guide to host your own dinners. The key is to start with a few key people in your network, invite them to connect, add value to their connections, and you'll get back tenfold what you invested. For those thinking they have to invest a small fortune to pull this off, Jayson will tell you pizza and wine (or your beverage of choice) at your home works just fine. It's not the amount of the tab that makes the mastermind dinner a success but the connections you create. His words of wisdom: "A lot of people don't invest in their relationships because they can't peg an ROI to it. That's why a lot of people don't take it seriously." But as an influencer, you should!

Strategic Roundtables

Another type of event that is ideal to cultivate connections and provide additional resources to clients is a strategic roundtable. The purpose is to connect with influencers who are one degree of separation from the client or receiver of the service.

As an example Jennifer Peek who is an interim CFO. Her firm provides valuations for companies that are being sold and comprehensive presentation materials for business debt refinancing and acquisition. Jennifer's ideal roundtables consist of experts who are all consulting with business owners who're going through a transaction. These include business brokers, bankers, attorneys, and wealth advisors. In essence, they could provide complimentary services to the same client. It's a strategic alliance with everyone hanging out on the same island, so to speak. They are all solution-oriented services. They can choose to enter into joint ventures or to recommend or hire each other's services for specific engagements to suit their clients' needs.

A roundtable is different from a mastermind group. Mastermind groups are ideal when facing a specific challenge. Aligning with likeminded business owners who have faced similar challenges and opportunities can help with problem solving and accountability.

Connecting Adventures: Scott's story

Scott Wesley, a wealth adviser I know in Kansas City, turns trips into connecting opportunities. He invites clients and individuals who could be clients to go on fishing and hunting adventures. These are perfectly orchestrated so that the focus can be on relaxing and getting to know each other. Think sweatworking in the great outdoors over an extended period of time. Great things happen when you get people out of their typical element. According to Scott, companies have been formed during these trips. Even if you can't organize a bucket-list trip like Scott does for people in his network , you can organize local excursions to put people together. Going on a local adventure, trying something new together, and sweatworking can get folks out of the usual routine and create strong relationships that build influence.

Specialty Circles

Another option for increasing your influencer status is to organize a small group that meets regularly. It's up to you whether the group has a business or personal-interest focus. As an example, I was a co-creator of a group of professional women who share common interests, one of them being spirituality. It's not an industry-specific group because we aren't focusing on how many connections we can make for each other. To date, there are 14 of us, which is ideal for the dynamics we wanted to nurture. Keeping the group intimate is something we've all agreed on based on type of conversations we have. Even though the original intent of the group wasn't focused on business, the expertise of the people in this particular group resulted in the formation of a business partnership. We've also utilized each other's services and made connections that have resulted in business opportunities for the members.

The group meets once a month, typically over lunch but occasionally for a happy hour, too. It's a very relaxed format with a focus on food and quality conversations about how we can support one another best personally and professionally. Because we are all entrepreneurs, our schedules can be a bit hectic at times. It's not a requirement to attend every lunch, but we do expect the group to stay connected in other ways with calls, texts and emails to each other.

Facebook groups

Facebook groups give you another option for bringing people together virtually and creating a community. You have the option of creating secret groups as well as closed groups. Secret groups give you the ability to communicate privately with each other, and the group can't be found in a search. A closed group can be found by anyone on Facebook, but you have control over who can join because you have to accept their requests. Whether open or secret, you can use Facebook groups to ask each other for help and insight with business and personal situations and to share articles or quotations that may be of interest. Posting to the group's page is easier than sending an endless string of emails back and forth because those can easily turn into long email strings that are hard to keep up with.

The groups are easy to create. After you create the group page on Facebook, there are a few things you can do to help make the group successful. Create a custom URL for the group page and craft a compelling description to get people engaged (think of it as a value proposition for your group). Make sure the group page is visible on your personal Facebook page so that it's easier for folks to find the group once they find you. Establish guidelines for membership and participation in the group, and enforce them diligently. Post content focused on a theme that ties into your connecting strategy. Finally, consider doing something special for the group like giving a free download or inviting the members to an event (depending on where the members are located) to keep them engaged and interested.

Just like with any social media forum, creating the group and doing nothing with it won't get you any results. It shows a lack of follow-through, which is a bad thing. Build the group slowly but surely by inviting and adding value to the folks who are strategic to what you're looking to accomplish and who would benefit from connecting.

A Business Model

George Weyrauch is an island alliance of mine. He's taken perfectly planned collisions and turned them into a business model as the Founder the of Rock Creative Network. He calls himself the Relationship Evangelist because he started his company to connect creative and marketing professionals with companies who need help creating awareness for their products or services. The companies he represents cover a broad range of creative services and he uses his 25 years of experience in advertising, branding and marketing to be the matchmaker between companies and agencies and marketing executives. As George says, his "company is like the eHarmony of creative."

As a super-connector with influence, you have numerous options for pulling people together. Whether you decide to organize a happy hour event, mastermind diner, a book club, wine club, a sweatworking gym "meeting," or a shared adventure, the options are numerous. Start by deciding whether you're organizing this alone or want alliances to help. Pick your date well in advance. Pay attention to every detail of planning the event, facilitate amazing connections, follow up, and do it again.

THE CIRCLE OF TRUST

Super-connectors understand that trust is everything. Trust is the foundation that influential relationships are built on. When you trust someone, you will feel comfortable doing business with them. Trusting someone means you know that person will take great care of a client you refer. That, in turn, will reflect well on you. You don't have to worry that the introduction you made is going to lead to a train wreck.

Building trust takes time. It's not easy for everyone, especially folks who lack integrity. People who are unorganized may also leave you in the dust with a promise that's left unfulfilled. The follow-up process is critical in maintaining trust and influence. If you say that you will introduce someone but forget or lose the contact information, that lack of follow-through erodes trust and, depending on the situation, can even create a landslide.

It's important to test the waters early on when making an introduction because every connection is a direct reflection on your reputation. It's one thing to meet people, decide you like them, and then get to know them. To be an effective influencer, you have to trust the people you allow into your network. You can meet people, like them, and take the time to get to know them. But you have to trust them, too. Never introduce someone to your best client or best friend for that matter, until you've seen that person in action. Introduce them to someone else first to make sure that they understand what connecting is about. Remember, the introductions you make and how you make them will directly reflect on who you are and how influential you can be. You're teaching people how you like introductions to be made.

Whether you're the conduit for an introduction or the person who's looking for a mutual connection to make an introduction on your behalf, consider how strong your relationship is with that person. Have you spent time nurturing the relationship by staying in contact with that person on a regular basis, or is your relationship more casual? If you sent me a message on LinkedIn that said, "Hey, there's someone who wants to meet you," but I don't know you at all, why would I accept that invitation? Clarity about your value is key. Influencers need clear reasons for making introductions, not casual requests.

Before making an introduction, always speak with both people to make sure this is a right-place-right-time connection. Do some research to about both people and be strategic about why these two people need to meet. Pick up the phone and have a conversation with each of them. Ask, "Is this a good introduction for you?" Give them a little background information on each other. Highlight the value of the connection. Help them understand why you think it could develop into a potential client relationship, a source of information, or even a friendship. You can't be upset if they say the introduction you're looking to make wouldn't be a good fit. Sometimes, they may already have the resources or connections they need or they don't have time to add more friends to their social calendars. They may also be closed-minded and not understand relationships, or the timing may simply be off.

HELPING INFLUENCERS COLLIDE

When you use your influence to put two people together, you're building trust and establishing yourself as a true super-connector. Here's a story I love sharing about what can happen when Bob Burg's go-giver philosophy brings two influencers together. When Bob Burg was in Kansas City, I introduced him to Harry S. Campbell. Harry was mentored by Sam Walton early on in his career. He was in top leadership at Sprint and is the current CEO at Durrie Vision. Everyone who's ever worked for Harry will tell you he is the epitome of a leader who walks his talk. He has written a book titled *Get-Real Leadership* and is working on his second book. I had an intuitive feeling that Harry and Bob needed to meet, but I didn't feel the need to be in the middle. As I was talking with Harry about the making the introduction, he shared that he would talk about Bob in his keynotes and hold up a copy of *The Go-Giver* for the audience to see it.

Since Bob was traveling, I coordinated a location and time that was convenient for both of them and let them have a conversation. Since then, Bob has interviewed Harry for a post on his blog. He invited him to speak at several events, and they remain in contact. The introduction had nothing to do with sales. It was done simply with the intent of introducing two of my favorite people on the planet.

Both have thanked me on several occasions for putting them together. Giving without the expectation of receiving can pay off in ways you never imagined, and if feels great!

When you're looking at making influential strategic connections, consider:

- The type of clients or connections both people are looking to make.
- Are they already in the same circles and just haven't met yet, or are they looking to expand their networks?
- What are their mindsets about creating relationships?
- Are they rock stars at what they do and providing stellar service?
- Do they actually follow up?

Once you've spoken to both parties, follow up with an email for the official introduction. Here's an example of one that I use. It's general in nature, so if there is a particular challenge one of them is facing, a resource one of them needs, etc. be sure to spell that out clearly in the email. The names of people, job titles, companies, and contact information are in bold so that you can spot them easily and change them to suit your needs.

Hello **Marsha** & **Jon**,

The world is a better place when great people connect.

Marsha, I'd like to introduce you to **Jon**, who works at **XYZ Company**. He's always looking to provide the best resources for his network. The two of you share a similar focus when it comes to the clients you serve. I've had the good fortune to know Jon for several years, and I know he will make you look good with any connections he can make for you.

Jon, Marsha is the **head of marketing** at **XYZ Bank**. We were recently introduced through **my colleague Jamie Smith**. It was easy to see why **Jamie** spoke so highly of **Marsha**: she understands the value of creating meaningful relationships. There are always opportunities when meeting with **Marsha**, and I know the two of you will benefit from connecting.

It appears there are potential opportunities between your circles of influence, so I would suggest scheduling coffee or lunch in the near future. In the meantime, your contact information follows. It includes your LinkedIn profiles so that you can get acquainted.

Name

Phone

Email

LinkedIn profile link

Name

Phone

Email

LinkedIn profile link

I trust the two of you can take it from here.

All the best,

Joyce

There are some who will copy you on the email conversation and others who won't, so you don't know how things progressed. Even though you've said, "I trust the two of you can take it from here," true super-connectors circle back around to make sure the conversation or meeting happened and was successful. Be sure you're tracking all introductions made by the date they initially happened, any correspondence between the people being introduced, and the result of the meeting.

Always thank people who make introductions for you. Pick up the phone, or send a note or an email. Acknowledging their efforts is a must, and they will be more inclined to make future introductions when they see that you get what connecting is about. If for any reason they haven't been doing this for the folks who've given them introductions, you've shared a gem with them by showing them an opportunity to build the relationship through gratitude.

#CONNECTINGHACK

Each time I write an introduction email for someone, I cut and paste the contact information as it's listed in the email into the notes section of their profile in my CRM. This makes writing introductions for those individuals easier the next time you make a connection for them. You can also include the introduction language you created in the email. This way, it's a simple cut-and-paste with a few tweaks for future introductions. No need to reinvent the wheel each time.

A DOUBLE DOUBLE COLLISION

Cameron Herold embodies all the qualities of a giver. If his name isn't familiar to you this might help. Cameron was the COO of the world's largest residential junk-removal company 1-800-GOT-JUNK? He's a sought after speaker to Young Presidents Organization (YPO), Entrepreneurs' Organization (EO) and Vistage groups. He's the author of *Double Double*, and his TEDx talk, "Let's Raise Kids to be Entrepreneurs," has over 1 million views. His advice: "Start building a network of fellow entrepreneurs that understand your passion and don't make you feel guilty about always chasing it."

Cameron is now a mentor and coaches CEO's and their teams around the world. Needless to say, I was surprised when he commented on a Facebook post I made in the Mastermind Dinners Facebook group with an offer to make introductions to CEO's he knows in Kansas City. We hadn't connected before then, so it was a true online collision in action. And in turn, I immediately thought of what kind of value I could add to him. And I'm still in awe that he was willing to make those introductions.

CONNECT THE DOTS

There are times that a stellar connection will come through several folks before an introduction is made. As an example, Chris Batz with The Lion Group LLC, who is a recruiter for law firms and fellow tech-junkie, was introduced to me by Pascale Henn with Pascale Henn Business Law Advisors LLC. Pascale is a savvy business attorney who came to me through Howie Fleishcher, a high-net-worth financial advisor, at Renaissance Financial. All of these people are amazing at what they do, and they are also super-connectors. When you're making notes in your CRM, be sure to connect the dots by including any additional connections about who connected you to this person. Show appreciation for their efforts with a quick phone call (a great way to reconnect, if you haven't spoken in a while), an email, or even a note. Along with the thank-you, ask if there's anything you can do for that person, like making an introduction to someone in your network. In minutes, you've strengthened your most influential connections.

COOL KIDS

Charlie "Tremendous" Jones says, "You'll be the same person in five years except for the people you meet and the books you read." It goes for stellar online connections as well. Think about who you want to surround yourself with. Being surrounded by successful and influential people is my goal. That's the perfect formula for being a cool kid.

If you're new at building your network and don't feel you have the connections or influence to be a cool kid, change your mindset. Even the most successful people in business and super-connectors started somewhere. Just ask Bob Burg or Jayson Gaignard. When I was in high school, I was far from a cool kid. I didn't hang with the popular folks and certainly didn't have athletic ability, at least not with organized sports. I felt like I was the furthest thing from being a cool kid.

In my TEDx talk, I shared a story that I'd never shared on stage before. I was in a verbally abusive relationship for over five years. It took a lot to find my confidence after that. Networking wasn't natural to me, and I stumbled a lot. I had to get out of my own head and comfortable in my business skin, so to speak. Looking back, I've come so far but still have far to go. I'm blessed with a network of fantastic people in my life. I had to take it one connection at a time, and as I experienced amazing synergies, connecting became easier. Folks call me a super-connector, but I'm just humbled at the people I've been fortunate to meet and opportunities that have come my way.

If you get to a point in your career, your life, and say, "I'm just done. There's no need to make another connection," you're missing opportunities. It isn't just about you. There could be someone you know who needs a resource you have influence with, or you could be the connection to a potential client. And sometimes those connections are outside the box.

On a recent business trip to Florida, I was sandwiched between two teenage brothers who both played football. The older brother, Michael, told me he is currently playing football at a small college. He had been playing left tackle and they had switched him to tight end. If you understand football, this is a difficult position change to make. He was frustrated to the point of quitting and coming back to Kansas City to enroll at a local community college with the goal of walking on the football team at the University of Kansas or Kansas State. It just so happens that I was introduced to Jon McGraw a year ago via Howie Fleischer from Renaissance Financial. Jon had a successful NFL career and played safety for the Kansas City Chiefs. He retired from football in 2011 and co-founded, Vision Pursue, a company that focuses on work in emotional intelligence. Being a retired NFL player puts him the cool-kid status, especially for Michael. I wasn't sure if there was a connection but thought it was worth exploring.

I asked Michael if he was open to a conversation with Jon for potential guidance since Jon had walked on at Kansas State. He said yes, so I gave him a business card. I knew he'd be out of pocket for a bit since he was on vacation with his family. He called me, which is more than I can say for some folks I've met in business when I offered them an introduction.

I sent Jon an email asking if he would be open to talking to Michael. He said he wasn't sure what kind of wisdom he could offer but was willing to talk to him. His willingness to have a conversation just reinforces his cool kid status!

Being able to see valuable connections is the difference between being just a networker and being a super-connector. Be prepared to step out of your comfort zone and make new connections, because you never know when the opportunity will arise. Cool kids care about the people in their networks. They think of the value they can provide, and they know that in order to receive, they first must give. They believe in reaching out just to stay in touch and focus on relationships that are mutually beneficial for everyone.

No matter where you start in life, everyone has the potential to be a super-connector, influencer, and cool kid.

ACTION

Decide the top three things you are taking action on after reading this chapter. Complete the Fast Start as quickly as possible. This will spark your internal motivation to tackle the other two.

Fast Start

One-Hour Win

Snail It

CHAPTER 8

RESPECTFUL RETREATS AND GRACEFUL EXITS

You can find a lot of information about creating new connections not just in this book but elsewhere. It's the topic of ending them that often goes unmentioned because it's a bit uncomfortable. But for super-connectors, knowing the art of respectful retreats and graceful exits is a must.

At the beginning of a relationship—whether personal or business—the people involved are putting a lot of work in. They're each putting their best foot forward to show how much they value and appreciate one another. Unfortunately, that it's not always the same when the relationship is ending.

Did you know that when you spend time with people who have bad attitudes or chronic bad moods, the odds dramatically increase that you can suffer from these, too? It's a phenomenon called social contagion. Research by medical sociologists Nicholas A. Christakis and James H. Fowler indicates that your odds of becoming unhappy increase by seven percent if you have just one unhappy friend.

When you're in a bad relationship, you're wasting time and energy that you could be spending on the people and pursuits that you enjoy. In business, you might need to end a relationship if:

- Someone you referred does a lousy job of service and follow-up with your client (this is why research is important).
- A business partnership goes sideways.

- A client costs more to work with in time, money, and frustration than they're worth.

- Someone behaves in a way that lacks integrity and damages his or her own reputation, and it begins to influence your relationships and how people see you.

- An employee no longer contributes any benefits to the company.

- A connection turns out to be an "energy vampire"—someone who sucks the life out of you.

- A connection turns out to be "pigeon." Pigeons seem harmless at first, but they have a tendency to make a mess by pooping on everything, and pigeon poop sticks like glue.

Too many people stay in bad relationships. They continue to put up with toxic, unpleasant, and unproductive associations because they don't want to hurt anybody's feelings. Sometimes, they just don't want to have the difficult conversation that it takes to actually end the relationship. But if you stay in a bad relationship, you'll pay a price in energy and happiness for having that person in your life.

Some people think that if they end a relationship, they've failed in some way. But look at the accountability factor. You've heard the saying, "It takes two to tango." Everyone has some accountability in a relationship. As easy as it is to blame yourself or the other person, consider what both of you brought to the table. Blaming everything on one person or the other ignores accountability for both.

Ending a bad relationship isn't selfish, because when you let go of the things that no longer serve you, then you have the time to focus on what's important: your goals and the positive people in your life, especially your island alliances, who actually deserve your attention.

If Jim Rohn is right that we are the average of the five people whom we spend the most time with, then your relationships will affect what your hopes and goals are for yourself. Consider what you want your career to look like. Think about what you want your life to look like. Who are the people who are helping you reach new levels of achievement? Think about the people who are *not* helping you move towards this vision. If you have a person in your life who fits that description, you may want to consider ending that connection.

SECOND CHANCES

When somebody's actions aren't what you think they should be or don't seem to be contributing much to your life, that's not a cause for you to end the business relationship and want that person out of your life immediately. Some people deserve a second chance.

When my mother was in a nursing home, my life was a little bit turned upside down because I was on-call 24/7 for her. I was in a constant juggling act to find new business, deliver to existing clients, and maintain sanity when my day could change in an instant. The people who knew me well knew that there were times when I would have to drop everything to take care of my mom because she was the most important person in my world at that time. My friends understood that client relationships had to be in second place because, since I work for myself, I needed to serve them. My friends and family were extraordinarily supportive of me and my mother at that time. They knew that I couldn't devote as much time to them as I wanted to. If I had an exceptionally bad day and just wasn't at the top of my game, they were understanding and patient.

If things aren't going well in one of your relationships, consider whether there was a hiccup in the other person's personal life. If it pertains to business, is what that person did *that* bad, or was it just a momentary bad judgment? Is this an isolated incident, or is it the connection's M.O.? What does your gut tell you? If something doesn't feel right, then listen to that gut reaction. Has the other person done anything to make things right, or has the situation been ignored? Actions always speak louder than words. If there's some way that the person could do something differently to improve the relationship going forward, have a conversation about that. You don't want to just walk away.

BURNED BRIDGES

That said, there are some relationships that you do just need to walk away from.

How you choose to handle a respectful retreat or graceful exit from a relationship can directly reflect upon your reputation and influence your future. You never know when six degrees of separation can turn into one. The person you burned a bridge with today may tomorrow be the person you're selling to or the person who can make an introduction for you.

If you have a personal relationship that goes sideways but the two of you share mutual business connections, have a conversation about how you will share the news with those mutual connections and continue doing business in the future. This is especially important if you plan on maintaining that connection.

When it came to online dating, I always approached potential connections with an open mind. If we weren't a fit for dating, then business was also an option. Sometimes, ending a personal relationship while maintaining a business relationship can be beneficial for both of you. Once, I was introduced to a guy through a mutual friend. After going out for a few months, I realized there was a friendship connection but not a heart connection. However, I had opened the door to several business opportunities for him, and he'd made a great introduction for me as well. After we had "the talk," he said, "You know, I've never dated a woman, broken up, and then actually maintained a business relationship." There's always a first time for everything!

How you handle ending a relationship speaks volumes about you and how you value connections. Yes, feelings might get hurt. But look at the good that can come out of ending something that isn't working and the lessons that can be learned. Ask yourself whether it's ultimately worth keeping someone in your life if you share mutual connections. Is it possible to work together after a separation?

If you decide to end a relationship, use Bob Burg's principles of "ultimate influence" to develop a strategy for approaching "the talk." As Bob explains in his book *Adversaries into Allies,*

Ultimate influence is based on five key principles that occur on an ongoing basis. In any interpersonal transaction where you desire to move a person to a different thought or action that they otherwise would take without your influence, you'll need to do one or more of the following:

1. Control your emotions
2. Understand the clash of belief systems
3. Acknowledge their ego
4. Set the proper frame
5. Communicate with tact and empathy.

Adversaries into Allies is about people skills, and understanding powerful people skills is important not just to succeed in life but especially for making a graceful exit without burning bridges.

BAD BUSINESS

Sometimes, business partnerships may go sideways. And frankly, some of them require attorneys to sort things out. No matter whether you are the one choosing to end it or are the one on the receiving end of the news, the way you approach ending a bad business relationship depends on what type of relationship it is.

When it's a relationship with a client, make sure you take care as you are letting go. And there are times when you may get dumped by a client, as well. You want to make sure that you do not end any kind of relationship in a haphazard way. You want to do this with respect and care no matter what the other person chooses to sling your way.

Social media presents special problems when relationships with clients go bad. You never know what might erupt if you get into a dispute with a client online. That dispute could take on a life of its own. Not long ago, the story of Amy's Baking Company Boutique & Bistro's "brand meltdown" meltdown went viral. The restaurant was featured in an episode of Gordon Ramsey's *Kitchen Nightmares* in which Ramsey declares the restaurant's owners, Samy and Amy Bouzaglo, too difficult to work with. The owners took to their Facebook business page in hopes of defending themselves against nasty comments being made by fans of the show. It turned into a PR disaster. The more comments the owners made, the nastier the responses got. Users on the social media platforms Yelp and reddit joined the escalating situation, too. As the mess spun further and further out of control, Amy's Baking Company claimed that their social media pages were hacked and that they were not responsible for the comments on their page. Yeah, right. Don't be them, no matter what!

If you're dealing with a client, don't rant on social media. Be aware that if you treat people unfairly in your business, they have the potential to rant on social media. And that's the last thing that you want to happen, because then other people who don't know all the facts may chime in. If things get heated, then you'll have a mess to clean up. Do your best to work through any difficulties in person. Truly, if you can't say something nice, then don't say anything at all.

If you have strategic resource partners (or suppliers) whose services you no longer need, the same rules apply. You hope they understand the reasons for the change, but in some cases, business turns to sour grapes. If they choose to be rude, stop returning calls, increase your rates, or take you out of "preferred client status," they're just shooting themselves in the foot because the odds are low that you'll ever choose to do business with them again. It's not just a future relationship with you that they've put in jeopardy but also anyone you know who could've used their services. If you're the resource partner or supplier whose services are no longer needed for whatever reason, then treat your former client with respect and understanding. You'll be leaving the door open for future business.

How much energy do you want to waste on being negative, anyway? If you happen to be the one being dumped in a business partnership, it can certainly take you off guard. Many people choose to start business partnerships so that they can combine talents or benefit from the others' expertise and connections. Some partnerships stand the test of time while others end because one partner starts to see flaws. It could be that one partner is more invested in the success of the company and works more hours. Or perhaps one partner decides that parting is the best choice because poor financial decisions are being made or communication is non-existent.

The best way to handle a breakup is to prepare for a potential breakup when you're starting the relationship. Think of it as a business pre-nup. You can define the details of how the split would happen in your company's operating agreement. If it's a loose partnership in name only with no combined assets, you still need to have some sort of plan in place. At least talk about it. If you can't have the conversation, you may want to consider whether the relationship is truly in your best interest.

Vindictive behavior isn't going to get you anywhere. It's been said that you can catch more bees with honey than with vinegar. When you're looking to make a graceful exit, that should be your priority. If you're feeling overly emotional or if you're feeling vindictive, keep your opinions to yourself and don't do anything that you're going to regret—privately or publically—because, after all, six degrees of separation can unexpectedly become two or even one.

It's best to have "the talk" in person if you can. Do *not* do it via email. Pick up the phone or meet in person because if people can't hear your tone of voice in your message, they can easily perceive things incorrectly, and that can cause even more hurt and trouble. When you have that conversation, do your best to keep a level head. Yelling isn't going to accomplish anything, and a condescending attitude never helps. Do your best to listen if you are meeting in-person. And if you happen to get emails flying back and forth, it may be helpful to get an outside opinion. Find someone whose opinion you trust and value who's not emotionally invested in the relationship. Ask them for an objective opinion and be willing to adjust the language if they say you need to.

As you're wrapping things up, don't forget the details, including the announcement of a parting, forwarding of contact information, and website updates to reflect the change. If there are any outstanding invoices, make sure your final bills are fair. It's wise to send out billing emails with specific instructions about when the payment is due. The language will depend on whether you're dealing with accounts payable at a large organization or an individual. If you're looking for clarity about how an invoice will be paid, you might use language like this example:

"In terms of payment, I want to be sure that we are on the same page, since we've had an opportunity to discuss the issue of invoicing. I anticipate that all outstanding amounts due will be received by (date). Please confirm your agreement. If not, please provide a payment schedule, so I can plan accordingly."

THE OTHER SHOES

If you're the one delivering unexpected news, be as kind as possible. This is tough to do, and a lot of people avoid conversations like this. If you're that kind of person, it may take some preparation on your part to make sure that your head is in the game. Put yourself in the other person's shoes. It's a big change either way, whether you're the one making the conscientious decision to end a relationship or you're the one on the receiving end of the news. It's our internal wiring that makes change feel uncomfortable and awkward for everyone involved. If you've been dealing with someone else's crazy behavior or working in a toxic environment, there's still a shift that has to take place. It sounds like a positive change, but if you've been in the situation long enough, your subconscious has gotten used to it. When we're under stress and pressure, we have a tendency to snap back to our normal or to what's comfortable. It's the very reason people who are in abusive relationships easily go back to another abuser versus the good guy. Everyone handles change differently so be aware of this for all involved.

People are hardwired to resist change, and it's even harder for them when it comes completely out of the blue. When you have that tough conversation, you want to be mature and professional. That means managing your emotions and being mindful of the other person's feelings. Before you have the conversation, mentally rehearse it. Bounce what you're going to say off somebody you trust to get feedback.

Do not assume that you know what the other person's response will be. We tend to make up stories of how we think things are going to go, and that ends up being exactly what happens. You want to make sure that you're not creating too many worst-case scenarios in your head. If you find yourself in a loop of negative self-talk, ask yourself if the stories you're telling yourself are true or if they're just your projections of what you think the outcome will be. Keep your mindset positive and your focus on the best possible outcome for the situation.

One way to keep your focus on the positive is to be thankful that this person has been in your life. If that person is someone you know through mutual connections, then there was a reason that you were introduced to begin with, whether it was as a client, a referral partnership, or a friendship. Thank the person for what they've done for you. If you can't deliver the thanks in person, write a letter to clear the air and to let those emotions go.

POSTMORTEMS AND BLAME-SESSIONS

Postmortems—pausing to reflect on the outcome of a situation—are an ideal way to see what went right, what went wrong, and—most importantly—what you need to do differently in future relationships so that you don't get into similar situations again. It's a more intense version of the "liked best" and "next time" mentioned earlier. Postmortems can help you figure out why you didn't get the job or why things didn't work out the way you hoped so that you can formulate a more effective plan for the future. Depending on the situation you're reviewing, postmortems can be useful to do by yourself or with your partner or your team.

Some folks consider postmortems to be little more than blame-sessions, but that's far from the point. The intent is not to just focus on the bad but to celebrate the successes you've had along the way. This is your opportunity to be accountable and admit how you contributed to the relationship that's ending. Stick to the facts and steer clear of emotions as they can cloud your judgment. Use what you learn from the postmortem to move forward in a positive light. Dwelling on what didn't work in the relationship will only take you further into negativity bias.

If you've recently walked away from a bad business relationship or a personal connection who brought more negativity than positivity to your relationship, doing a postmortem before the next client, partnership, or connection is critical. It requires you to take time for reflection so that you don't jump into another new situation only to repeat your mistakes. You'll also be able to look back on the relationship with more clarity and honesty than you might have been able to when you were in it.

Ask yourself (and your partner or team) the following questions in your relationship postmortem:

- How did things go?
- What didn't go as well as I/we wanted it to?
- Do I/we keep doing what's always been done, or have I/we challenged assumed knowledge and tried new approaches to problems?
- Do I/we proactively seek new challenges, or do I/we just manage existing challenges?
- How could I/we improve the outcome next time, if given the opportunity?

Use any negativity that's left to propel yourself forward to the goals and visions that you're focused on, and do it with a smile. Your reputation is affected not just by the feeling people get when they're with you but by the feeling they get when you walk away. So, when you're exiting a relationship, use the exit as an opportunity to build your reputation for being someone who can handle tough situations gracefully and respectfully. As Molière said, "It is not only what we do, but also what we do not do, for which we are accountable."

BREAKING UP IS HARD TO DO

Don't go into a relationship blindly. It's easy to put on rose-colored glasses at the beginning of a relationship. As much as you feel "in love" with your island alliances, clients, resource partners or employees, do some research on them first—whether it's via web or mutual connections—to make sure that getting into the relationship is a good decision. Think about every possible relationship and business outcome. If this is a partnership you're diving into and legal documents need to be filed, it's going to take more to dissolve that kind of relationship. There are no guarantees, but at least you've done your part.

No matter the type of relationship, commit to having open, honest conversations, even the difficult ones. Be willing to respectfully disagree with someone instead of keeping silence that harbors resentment, which will only build over time.

"Breaking Up Is Hard to Do": A great song for those of us who remember 1960's classics. But with respectful retreats and graceful exits, you can be sure to keep your reputation and your sanity intact.

ACTION

You're at the end of another chapter, so it's time to decide what you will take action on.

Fast Start

One-Hour Win

Snail It

CHAPTER 9

STRATEGY-SETTING, PRIORITY-PLANNING AND ISLAND LAWS

You may have heard about the 1953 study done at Yale in which graduating seniors were asked if they had written down the specific goals they wanted to achieve in life. Twenty years later, the researchers tracked down the same group of students and found that three percent of those who had specific goals throughout those two decades had accumulated more personal wealth than the other 97 percent combined.

This study has been referenced countless times by trainers, consultants, and motivational speakers as the reason you need to set personal goals. Well, there's a small catch to the study. After extensive research, the *Fast Company* Consultant Debunking Unit (CDU) found that the study's conclusions are completely untrue, and the CDU published an article in December 1996 to support their findings. According to the article—titled "'If Your Goal is Success, Don't Consult These Gurus"—the CDU went directly to the source: retired lawyer Silas Spengler, who is also the secretary of the Class of 1953. According to Spengler, he never wrote down any personal goals, nor did he and his classmates ever participate in a research study on personal goals.

If you've been writing goals for your entire life or your entire career at the end of each chapter of this book and filling out the action steps, you'll be relieved to know that there was a study done by Gail Matthews at Dominican University of California in 2007 involving more than 200 participants that provides empirical evidence to support the effectiveness of accountability, commitment, and writing one's goals down.

As stated in the introduction, four of the most dangerous words in the English language are, "I already know that." You can intellectualize it and talk about it, but unless you're taking action, it doesn't count for much. Getting specific about what your goals are and how you plan to achieve them will keep you focused on achieving them. The exercises in this book have been designed to help you get specific about what you already know, along with new information gained that you can apply to your connecting advantage strategy.

YOGI BERRA STRATEGIES

Yogi Berra once said, "If you don't know where you are going, you will likely end up somewhere else." Strategy has been a recurrent theme throughout the book. If you don't know what you want—personally and professionally—you'll have a hard time making it happen. Clarity is key. You'd be surprised at how many people don't have strategies to guide them, let alone objectives or specific goals. To create a strategy, you don't need to do an in-depth SWOT analysis. You can start by simply asking yourself:

- What is the vision for your career? This is your big-picture view, your hopes and dreams.

- What are the your short-term goals for your career? Do they include growing your business, making a career shift, shifting within your current company, finding more clients, etc.?

- What do you need the most help with achieve your immediate goals?

- How urgent are the goals?

- What is your timeframe for achieving those goals?

- Why do you want to achieve your goals? Think past money and focus on what motivates you to make success happen. If you don't have a reason, any little hiccup in your plan might cause you to give up.

- What are you looking to accomplish in your personal life over the same timeframe? What are your priorities for your interests, hobbies, volunteer work, etc.?

- Is there anything that you need to do differently to make your goals happen? What new habits, beliefs, actions, etc., will help you on your way?

- Who could potentially help you execute those steps?

Once you have clarity about what your vision, goals, and needs are, you can be more strategic about creating connections that will help you make your goals a reality.

Before you start making new connections, ask yourself, "Who is it that I *already* know? Who is it that I *want* to know?" Looking through your current list of contacts is a great place to start answering those questions. If your contacts are in a CRM and tagged by type of relationship, industry, etc., then it will be easy to search through them. If you're using excel spreadsheets, stacks of business cards, or post-it notes as a method of tracking your contacts, you'll have your work cut out for you.

TAKING YOGI ONLINE

LinkedIn is also a great tool for making a list of the people you're already connected to who are of strategic value to you. Think island alliances, resources and super-connectors. Use the search box at the top of the page to search for a person, a company, or a keyword related to what you want to find. As you're looking at somebody's profile, remember to look off to the right side of the page to see who else has similar backgrounds or interests. Keep notes about what you find to save time if and when you have to do the searches again.

There may be connections outside your current LinkedIn network who could also be helpful. For example, when I was looking for funding connections for my client, I did a simple keyword search on LinkedIn for individuals who listed "venture capital" and "private equity" on their profiles. The words were either in the headings or summary sections of their profiles. Once I found a potential connection, I did a Google search of that person's firm to ensure I was on the right track. If we shared a mutual connection, I reached out to see what my contact knew about them and whether they had any personal experience with that individual. If we didn't have any shared connections, I crafted a very short email to introduce myself.

Twitter also has a search option for names, hashtags, and keywords, which is also at the top of each page. You can search for specific people to see what they are posting. Or you can use this feature to pull up every tweet that mentions the words you searched. Whether it's in a person's twitter handle, hashtag, or in the tweet itself, you'll find them all in a search. For example, the results I got when I searched for the words "business strategy" included the following profile: "@BusinessInsider. The latest business advice and strategy." It also showed me tweets like "9 science-backed signs you're smarter than average bit.ly/0w7tlK1 #business #strategy."

#CONNECTINGHACK

A great tool for monitoring Twitter for updates about things and people who're related to your strategic search terms is Twilert. They'll also search for terms that are key to your brand and your company's brand. You can expand your network by following folks who show up in search results and then sorting them into your Twitter lists. It takes a few extra seconds, but it's worth adding experts who post relevant content about your strategy, relevant folks and experts to specific lists for future reference and, of course, retweets!

Commun.it is another great hack for Twitter and Facebook. It helps you to identify valuable members of your community to better manage your relationships. From your biggest fans to customers and influencers, Commun.it will help you to stay connected and increase engagement.

STAYING PLUGGED IN

Part of accomplishing your goals is being plugged into what's going on in your city. Reading the local newspaper may give you some information, but I'm referring here more to magazines and other business publications that could be helpful in finding connections and relevant information resources. Business journals are published in most cities across the U.S.. Do a quick Google search for business publications in your city to see what options you have. In Kansas City, we have magazines like *Ingram's* and *Kansas City Business Journal,* and *Thinking Bigger Business Media*. Not only did the founder, Kelly Scanlon, build a terrific magazine—*Kansas City Small Business Journal*, which is now *Thinking Bigger Business Media*—she expanded the company's reach with events including the 25 Under 25 Awards. Knowing about what business leaders in your community are doing can help you discover new possibilities for meeting the people you want to meet and getting access to the resources you're looking for.

If you're looking for more social connections rather than business connections, you'll still need to think about the people that you want to connect with and the resources that you need. Are you looking for a cycling group, a group for new mothers, or is there a specific volunteer organization that you want to get in contact with? Do a little research based on your strategy. Use your contact lists to help make your list. If your RAS is tuned into your strategy, you'll be able to see social opportunities while you're also finding business connections. You might find a way to make a strategic connection to someone who shares your interests by reading about who won a business award or whose business is profiled in a business journal. Once you've found who or what you're looking for, keep track of the information in your CRM.

Before reaching out to make that connection, do a quick check to be sure your brand is ready to represent you. Use chapter one as a guide for making sure that your brand is consistent across all platforms with contact information that makes it easy for someone to find you. You may be the one searching, but you never know who will find you in the process. Also, make sure that your value proposition is clearly defined and ready to articulate in an email or face-to-face meeting.

REFINING, REVISING AND REVISITING

When it comes to connecting online and offline, what do you feel you are really good at? Is there anything essential to your strategy that you are still uncomfortable with? These are things that you need to think through. If there's something you're uncomfortable doing, then what can you do to shift your mindset to help stretch your comfort zone?

If there's something you find yourself procrastinating about or, worse yet, absolutely hate, like posting content to social media, is it possible for you to hire somebody to do it? If whatever you're avoiding is part of your strategy and is integral to building your business, then you have a decision to make. Typically when someone sees value in an activity, that solves the procrastination issue. If you have a fear of technology, then reading a book may not solve the problem. If the task is going to take you three times longer to do it than someone else, it may not be worth the time and cost compared to what you could be earning on other high-payoff activities. When you look at an hour of your time, what is the return on investment?

If attending an event still makes you feel uncomfortable, but you are the person who needs to go, re-read chapter three. The four inches between your ears can be your best ally or your worst enemy. The good news is that you are in control of it!

Be deliberate about choosing networking events to attend. What type of events are most valuable to you? How many networking events do you want to attend? Hint: the answer is, "Not every one." How often will you attend networking events? How are you going to track where you're going, how often you're going, and what your results from attending?

Once you find the most productive events for you, suit up and show up consistently, or else you could be out of sight and out of mind. Consistency is key! Once-a-year guest appearances at networking events aren't going to cut it.

It's easy to stay in our comfort zones with our connections, too. Being specific about the people that you want to meet is a must, but so is diversifying your connections. Too often, our ideas about who can help our career endeavors are too limited. If you're a real estate agent, your network shouldn't only consist of mortgage brokers. If you're not open to meeting a range of people, you may discount key connections who could open new doors and present unexpected opportunities. Having a diverse network is also relevant for folks who are making career transitions. If your network is focused in one industry and you decide to change your career or seek a new position, your connections may be too limited to help you. Waiting until you need connections is the wrong strategy. It takes time to grow a network, so don't wait until you need a wider network to build diversity.

BUILDING RELATIONSHIP MUSCLE

No matter who is on your list of key connections—both existing relationships and newer ones—developing meaningful relationships takes time. One coffee or lunch meeting may not give you all the information that you need to form a relationship. At the beginning of the meeting, define what you both most want to accomplish to keep yourselves on track for the time that you have. If this is your first meeting, take a few minutes to get to know each other's background and maybe a few personal details too like family, hobbies, and special interests. It's easy to get caught up in the getting-to-know-you conversation and then run out of time to determine how you can best help each other. Asking clarifying questions about the type of clients you work with, the problems/challenges they hired you to solve, and services you provide are important. Ask if that person has strategic resources, suppliers, or other connections who have been valuable to his or her business. This is where your RAS should be highly tuned in to find overlaps in your services and that person's needs. Do you each compliment what the other has to offer? Are you competitors, or is this a cooperatition (cooperation and competition) opportunity? That is, do you have an overlap of services but could still potentially refer each other business or be sounding boards for each other with challenges you experience? Value is key, as you never know when you can open the door for someone or vice versa.

The more you connect others who are in line with your strategy, the more opportunities come back. So develop a time strategy for investing your time in strengthening connections. What you choose to do is up to you, but here are few suggestions if you don't know where to start.

Block 30 minutes once a week to post a recommendation to the LinkedIn profile of someone you know well. Send two emails a week to touch base with folks who've been on your mind. Make one phone call to someone whom you've been wanting to schedule coffee or lunch with. Social posts are another way to touch base and give props. If you're already blocking time for social media, then be sure to include a few extra minutes to share a post or article your connections have shared in their stream. Whether you're doing this on LinkedIn, Facebook, or Twitter, you'll be increasing your collision rate. If a post crosses your stream that you know is perfect to share with someone, take a minute and send it to that person. It could be in an email, text, or online message. Just sitting at your desk doesn't help you build relationships. If you're too busy to look up from your work and notice potential opportunities for others, then why should someone do that for you?

Recently, I met a business developer who doesn't see the value of spending any time on LinkedIn because it didn't work for that person's spouse. LinkedIn may not exactly be the field of dreams, but if you build a profile that's valuable to the people you want to connect to, they will come. It takes effort on your part—and, more importantly, the *right* effort—and as a way of strengthening connections, it's a strategy worth investing time in.

CLIENT INFLUENCE AND IMPACT

When it comes to enhancing connections with your current clients, don't focus solely on what you can sell them every time you talk to them. They may be less inclined to pick up the phone when you call. Think about how you can add value to those relationships. Do you know them and their needs well enough to know whether there are any resource partners you could introduce them to? Also ask who might be potential clients for them. What are their personal interests and needs? If you can do something for one of their children or family members, you'll be remembered fondly.

You might think that you already know the needs of clients and island alliances you've established business relationships with. But changes in your business—like the addition of a new product or service—are "connect worthy" and may be just the thing they need. Reaching out to established contacts about your changes may result in new business. Graphicmachine is a resource that I refer a number of clients to. Their expertise is in helping clients tell their story by creating a compelling brand and sharing it via website, video, social media and podcasts. I recently found out that one of the company's partners has been programming since age seven! This service perfectly aligns with the current work that they do. Instead of having to hire another company to solve technology issues, Graphicmachine is a one-stop-shop for their clients. The clients just need to know about it.

With the right outreach strategy, it's easy to reach out to existing customers and island alliances to find out what's new in their businesses, how their needs are changing, and how you might be able to help them. It's not always a sales-focused conversation. Asking great questions can help uncover ways you may be able to assist them. The last thing you want to hear is, "I wish you would have told me that last week. I just referred someone for that service." Life is short and time flies, so reach out regularly to the connections you value.

Don't forget to follow up promptly and consistently with new connections and to strengthen existing connections. A CRM is a valuable tool to help you determine the number of times you have reached out and when you need to be in contact again in the future. If you are in sales, you've probably heard the saying, "The fortune is in the follow-up." It doesn't matter your profession: connecting is all about the follow-up.

YOUR SOCIAL CALENDAR

In chapter seven, we looked at how sharing content that influencers post on social media platforms while you are *becoming* an influencer is key to connecting success. On LinkedIn, you can easily post content to your newsfeed or your company's page. You should also add a few insights of your own to the comments on LinkedIn articles posted by others. You can use the same strategies on Twitter, Facebook, your blog or company blog, and other social media platforms. Pinterest, YouTube, Google Hangouts, and podcasting give you even more options. Make sure you've chosen platforms that will help you reach the people you want to meet and that will benefit the goals you've set for yourself. Most importantly, *be consistent* on the platforms you choose to use. Use your calendar to set and keep a routine for posting content on the platforms you've chosen.

#CONNECTINGHACK

If scheduling and posting content seems a bit daunting, meet Edgar. Edgar is a social media scheduling tool. According to the Edgar website:

You write a social media update and upload it to Edgar, categorizing it for your library. Edgar posts it according to your category-based schedule. The update gets stored in your library. When every other update in that category has been posted, Edgar will post this one again, so it can be seen by a lovely new audience while you carry on worry-free.

Peter Drucker, a world renowned author and management consultant said, "If you can't measure it, you can't manage it." Measuring the influence of your social media posts will help you know the value of what you're sharing and the level of engagement you're getting from it, too. Keep in mind that the social aspect of your connecting strategy isn't just about the numbers of followers or posts you share. Pay attention to the folks who share your content. Their level of engagement will influence others to follow you as well as buy from you. Those folks can also eventually become advocates of your brand. If you're in a business development role, then keep track of the number of leads generated and meetings scheduled from the platforms you use. Notice the different types of content you post and which get the best results. The efforts may also pay off in invitations to participate on boards or other groups that are beneficial to your strategy.

Entrepreneur and *Forbes* contributor Ryan Westwood was recently interviewed on the Entrepreneur On Fire podcast, where he was asked an interesting question: what would he do if he had to start a new business from scratch with nothing but some cash and a laptop in hand? His advice: he'd "leave the laptop, go out and build relationships." Westwood went on to explain that social media is a valuable tool that can be used to make a connection or strengthen a connection. Ultimately, social media platforms "all lead back to people… The tech exists just to help you connect," not to be the connector. That's your job.

CONNECTING BOXES AND SHARK TANKS

Too often, people think of networking and they get tunnel vision by only looking at events instead of thinking about whom they'd like to meet and where might they be hanging out, both in person as well as online. The social media world increases your collision rate when you apply the right tactics. Think outside the box.

I jokingly refer to my friend Lea Bailes as a recovering attorney. He is a serial entrepreneur with a constant desire to learn and grow. Lea's clients include a host of startups and small- and mid-size businesses. I've seen the stellar results of his product launches, Facebook marketing strategies, and crowd-funding campaigns. We were talking at lunch recently about ways to make connections to successful startups. I had an outside-the-box suggestion that may provide opportunities for Lea to connect to startups: ABC's *Shark Tank*. The show features a panel of potential investors, called "sharks," who consider offers from aspiring entrepreneurs seeking investments for their business or products.

I'm an avid fan and enjoy watching the negotiations between the sharks and entrepreneurs or small business owners who are seeking funding for their business, products, or services. When you watch the show, you're only getting a portion of what is happening during the negotiations because the show is prerecorded. It's impossible to complete an entire business negotiation in 10 minutes. It may be "reality TV," but some of those negotiations would easily take an hour or more. If you're only watching what's on television, then you're missing a lot of the action behind the scenes.

On the nights that *Shark Tank* is airing live, I suggested to Lea that he check out their Twitter stream at the same time. Search for *#SharkTank* or #ABCSharkTank and you'll see a stream of conversations. Since the TV show is prerecorded, the Sharks—Barbara Corcoran, Daymond John, Mark Cuban, Robert Herjavec, Kevin O'Leary and Lori Greiner—are actually commenting on the show via Twitter. They're giving you the play-by-play that you didn't hear about when it was actually being taped.

Think about who typically would be watching *Shark Tank*: entrepreneurs and other business-minded folks, including those who want to be on the show with their own pitches. Look at who the sharks are mentioning and interacting with on Twitter. Clearly, those are individuals with influence, if they landed on the sharks' radar. Who else is commenting and getting a lot of retweets?

If you can watch the show at the time that it first airs, jump into the conversation by tweeting during the show. This will increase your collision rate and gives you the chance to make new connections. Set up a Twitter list just for *Shark Tank* so you know where and how you connected with contacts you interacted with in those conversations. Look at who is talking to whom and who is being retweeted. Always thank people for retweeting you.

Even if you can't watch the show live, that's ok. Once the show is over, you're still able to read through the stream to see who participated in the conversation. If you are extremely busy, but know that social media is a key part of your strategy, then you might consider hiring an assistant who is very savvy in the Twitterverse to help you out. Reach out to your current network to see if someone has a recommendation for an assistant you can hire. If you're a solopreneur who only needs help for a few hours a week, you can also look to a virtual assistant for this type of work. Upwork is a great online platform to post a job request to find virtual assistants, who can work remotely from literally anywhere in the world.

THE PRINCESS BRIDE GOES TO LINKEDIN

I'm a huge fan of the movie *The Princess Bride*. Originally released in 1997, it's since become a cult classic. Even if you haven't heard of the movie, there a number of raving fans, including my fellow Facebook friends. Not long ago, I saw a Facebook post that had a coffee cup that was a spinoff of Inigo Montoya's famous line in the movie: "Hello my name is Inigo Montoya, You killed my father, prepare to die." The coffee cup had a photo of a name tag that read "HELLO MY NAME IS Inigo Montoya. You drank my coffee, prepare to die." When I shared this on Facebook, I got more than 50 likes and comments and quite a few shares. Comments, shares, and likes show the level of engagement, and I'm constantly testing content to see what people find interesting. So I thought, "Why not test the waters on LinkedIn?" Since LinkedIn is a business platform, I usually post things related to business, but my Facebook friends have said that they follow me for motivation and humor. When I posted that image of the coffee cup on LinkedIn, I wrote, "Everyone needs a little humor in business."

The number of comments and likes that post got went through the roof. The LinkedIn Influencers with massive followings can get thousands of likes and comments. Even though I fall under the LinkedIn Publisher status and have the ability to post on that platform, my engagement level isn't quite as high as an Influencer's. It would take every person following me to comment to make that happen, so to get 29 likes and 27 comments on one post was a *big* deal! The interesting thing was that of all the comments posted, the majority of them were made by men who were citing lines from the movie. Who knew? Of course I had to chime in a few times too.

Then six degrees of separation kicked in. The president of a pharmaceutical company in California whom I wasn't directly connected to posted three different comments. The picture had shown up in his stream because a mutual connection in Kansas City had commented on it. I reached out with an invitation to the CEO and said, "Frankly, anyone who likes *The Princess Bride* is just cool. I welcome the opportunity to connect on LinkedIn and expand our networks." And he immediately accepted that invitation. Of course, all of this prompted a LinkedIn Publisher post titled "Assumptions, Questions & The Princess Bride."

Even though I used the same photo, the post I made didn't get as many comments as the original image, but my post was viewed 181 times with 24 likes. And I made sure to mention the people who have commented on the original picture to give them credit, as well. Since then, I've taken a slight sidetrack on occasion from the typical business posts with great results.

THOUGHT LEADERS AND TREND SHAPERS

What is a thought leader? Thought leaders are the people who have influence in determining what matters in their industry or social sphere. So why does thought leadership matter? Because there are so many other people who can do exactly what you do and are waiting in line for the chance to do it. You can easily get lost in a sea of vanilla. Whether you're being intentional about it or not, everything you post is a direct reflection of who you are and what you stand for. It speaks directly to your personal brand.

Thought leadership in a business market is even more critical because according to a talk given by Jamie Shanks and Tim Keelan at the SAVO Summit 2014, 74 percent of buyers choose the company that was the first to add value as they defined their buying visions. "Business buyers don't 'buy' your product or service," according to Jeff Ernst with Forrester Research, "they 'buy into' your perspective and approach to solving their problems." That means that thought leaders have a role in shaping the trends of their industries, which will also shape who their clients are and the services they provide to those clients.

In "The Golden Rules for Creating Thoughtful Thought Leadership," Daniel W. Rasmus writes that a thought leader's creative contributions "should be an entry point to a relationship. Thought leadership should intrigue, challenge, and inspire even people already familiar with a company. It should help start a relationship where none exists, and it should enhance existing relationships." This is the kind of leadership that can shape your perceptions about your brand and your business in the right way. When you can understand and answer the most important questions of your target audience, you become an authority and a thought leader.

Start by defining which type of thought leader you want to be:

- Industry Thought Leadership - news and trends
- Organizational Thought Leadership - vision and culture for your company
- Product Thought Leadership - solutions and best practices

Keep your strategy—your interests and your long- and short-term goals—in mind as you decide what kind of thought leader you want to be. Once you make that decision, you'll need to start sharing content that establishes you as a thought leader in your network. Don't know where to start when it comes to content? Consider the unique experiences or areas of expertise you can share. What makes you un-vanilla? What are the important influences in your life and career that have shaped you? What lessons have you learned that could benefit others?

In a video interview on BigThink, Dorie Clark shares the following insight on thought leadership:

> Some people think that they can't have a big idea; they can't be a thought leader because everything's already been done. They have an idea, but somebody else got there first. The truth is every idea has already been taken. That is no excuse not to do something about it...
>
> And the way that you do that is through stories and anecdotes that you hear and by something being conveyed from a particular perspective. You have something unique to offer by dint of who you are. Even if something in theory has been done before, it hasn't been done by you in the way that you can do it. It's time to step forward and to recognize that you can make a contribution.

Chapter two listed five questions from "Your Stand Out Self-Assessment: 139 Questions to Help You Find Your Breakthrough Idea and Build a Following Around It." If you haven't taken the time to go through all of the questions, now's the time to do it.

You don't have to be a best-selling author or keynote speaker to become a thought leader. If the idea of writing blog posts is overwhelming, then start by sharing timely content that your audience can use *now*. Look for something that can help them with an immediate situation or something that can prepare them for tomorrow's challenges. The key is to make the content relevant to your network. Numbers and statistics can tell your network a lot, for example, but thought leaders don't use just statistics alone to tell a story. They deliver a powerful and relevant message about those statistics that their audiences will remember.

As you're starting to share content, be forward-thinking. Time to push those comfort zones again! One idea or prediction can spark a conversation. TED talks use that format to launch innovative ideas, so why can't you? Consider what you've gained from your past experiences and lessons. Add that to your gut instinct and pose some powerful "What if?" questions to your audience.

You build your brand and thought leadership one post at a time.

#CONNECTINGHACK

If you're looking for a variety of content to share with your connections, LinkedIn SlideShare is a great resource. Sharing its educational, inspirational, and innovative content on a wide range of topics with your connections is easy to do with just the click of a mouse. Another resource that's great for finding valuable content is Scoop.it. This platform lets you aggregate content and publish what you've found in a single location, which makes sharing that information simple. You can use the scheduling feature to publish content on a regular schedule.

You can also use Help A Reporter Out (HARO) to register yourself or your business as a potential news source for journalists who're writing stories about your industry and are looking for experts and industry leaders

PRIORITIES AND BIGGER PICTURES

The strategy is the bigger picture. The next step is to prioritize the steps to make it happen. Putting effort into prioritizing what you need to do and where you need to spend your time will maximize the results of your goals and dreams. Making connecting a priority can determine the difference between success and struggle or stagnation. To get where you want to go in business and life takes preparation.

According to Brian Tracy, a sales training and success authority, "Every minute spent in planning saves as many as ten minutes in execution. It takes only about 10 to 12 minutes for you to plan out your day, but this small investment of time will save you up to two hours (100 to 120 minutes) in wasted time and diffused effort through the day."

The time you invest should be based on your goals and how you plan to get there from where you are currently. If you're in business development, then 50 percent of your time will be focused on building solid relationships. If you're in a job transition and you're already employed, then you'll need to carve out time to do some stealth job-seeking. If you're out of work, then connecting should be a full-time commitment. Looking for resource connections? That's less time-involved, but the steps are the same. If you're adding another "hat" to your job, then you'll need folks to help you make that happen.

If you're not doing it already, you may need to schedule 10-15 minutes a day to plan out your connecting agenda. Your agenda should include blocks of time for specific activities. Start with your workday and activities associated with it—meetings, projects, etc.— anything mission-critical to your work commitment. Once you have that time blocked, it's time to get serious about your connecting advantage. Go back to each chapter in this book and review your top-three action items. Which is the number-one item that you commit to taking action on today? Is it something you need to schedule, or can you pick up the phone for a quick call? Once you have your time "chunks" blocked, then you want to schedule time to create and implement the steps needed to complete more time-intensive items. Don't just let them sit there or keep putting them off. For example, I use Google Calendars and color-code my agenda, using a different color for speaking engagements, coaching clients, networking activities, one-on-one meetings, and "my time," which includes the gym and other activities (yes, plan for "your time," too). I can see at a glance where I'm spending the majority of my time.

If you can, schedule back-to-back meetings two days a week as well as uninterrupted office days. If I'm working on a project, I block that into my schedule, too. If ADD is an issue, then turn off your cell phone and log out of social media, email, etc. It may be a little uncomfortable at first, but it will pay dividends in the long run! Also, consider how you will track the return on your time investments and how they're helping you meet your goals.

For those who say, "I don't have any more time in the day," remember that you're adding to the problem by continuously telling yourself that. Think back to the exercise in chapter five and what you determined what your time is worth. Then think about how your time isn't spent effectively. What does it cost you every time you go to an event or a one-on-one meeting that was a complete waste of time because you didn't take five minutes to do a little research first? How much time do you spend watching TV? I agree there are times when one needs to completely veg out, but more often than not, TV is a time-suck. I got rid of my cable subscription for a year. When I actually had time to watch it, it was only to see what was on the DVR, and that was a week after the show aired. No cable meant that I had time to focus on the important things like going to the gym, feeding my mind with good stuff and reading the books on my ever-growing reading list. If you're unsatisfied with where you're at, then maybe you need to reconsider what you spend time on.

ISLAND LAWS AND STRATEGIC ALLIANCES

Friends and family are a given. Just don't forget to talk about your connecting goals over holiday dinner because you never know whom they know or how they may be able to help you. Don't assume, or you might miss an opportunity!

Your inner circle island alliances—the four to ten people whom you're closely aligned with—also help you make things happen. These are the connections who are always top-of-mind for you. Know who they're looking to meet and resources they need, too.

Your strategic alliance circle expands beyond your inner circle to include the people you turn to often and have taken the time to get to know. You also have a general understanding of how they can help you, who can possibly help them, and who would make good connections for them.

Keep a list (or tag them in your CRM) of eight to ten super-connectors whom you have a relationship with or want to develop a relationship with. Every 60 days or so, take out the list and evaluate your current relationship with each person on a scale of one to ten. For anyone who scores lower than eight, develop an action plan to improve your connection before your next review.

You want to focus on filling your island with people who embody a go-giver mindset and will support you in your endeavors.

Bob Burg and John David Mann's *The Go-Giver* includes a list of the "Five Laws of Stratospheric Success," which are excellent principles for maintaining your island alliances relationships:

1. The Law of Value: Your true worth is determined by how much more you give in value than you take in payment.

2. The Law of Compensation: Your income is determined by how many people you serve and how well you serve them.

3. The Law of Influence: Your influence is determined by how abundantly you place other people's interests first.

4. The Law of Authenticity: The most valuable gift you have to offer is yourself.

5. The Law of Receptivity: The key to effective giving is to stay open to receiving.

The laws bring new relevance to the old proverb "Give and you shall receive." Imagine if everyone operated under these laws.

When considering who's already on your island or on your list of potential island alliances, ask yourself the following questions, which I posed in a slightly different form in *Just Another Leap*:

- Do you encourage each other to set bolder goals and hold each other accountable?
- Do you help each other push comfort zones?
- Do you provide insight and inspiration that challenges you to be better versions of yourselves?
- Do you share similar values?
- Do you have fun when you are together? (This is very important!)
- Do you share a go-giver mindset?

If you don't answer yes to the majority of these questions about your island alliances, then some of them may not be a good fit for your island. That's not to say that you won't keep them in mind if an introduction would be appropriate, but they're just not hanging out with you on the beach roasting marshmallows, either. Nurture your alliances. Show them love. Spend time getting to know them.

And if for any reason you have to say good-bye, re-read chapter eight. It's the equivalent of a sign that reads: "In case of emergency, break glass."

GIVE AND TAKE

Adam Grant, Wharton's youngest tenured professor and author of *Give and Take*, expands on Carnegie's concepts in How to Win Friends and Influence People, and shows that success is increasingly dependent on how we interact with others. The basic premise of the book is that "givers" are more successful in the long-run for a variety of reasons. The variables of success that he focuses on are how people approach their attitudes and interactions with other people. Do they claim or contribute value, and what are their preferences for reciprocity? He categorizes people as takers, givers, or matchers. Takers are the kind of people who get more than they give, tilting reciprocity in their favor. Givers give more than they get, tilting reciprocity the other's direction. Matchers are interested in fairness and interacting in a way that balances reciprocity. It's interesting to note that individuals may shift their approaches depending on whether they're in a business or personal relationship. As an example, someone may be a giver with friends and family and a taker with coworkers.

Do you wonder how you actually rate when it comes to reciprocity? Adam created an assessment to test your giver quotient using state-of-the-art methods from organizational psychology. You have the option of taking a self-assessment to understand your reciprocity style. You can also take a 360-degree assessment to find out whether others see you as you see yourself. The data you receive will show how often you're seen as a giver, taker, or matcher. The 360-degree assessment must be taken by 10 people for accurate feedback.

The following link will take you to both assessments.

www.giveandtake.com/#!evaluateyourself/c10x3

The act of giving doesn't have to take vast amounts of time or resources. Adam Rifkin, co-founder of PandaWhale, and named best networker in Silicon Valley by *Fortune* in 2011, said, "It's who you know, not what, that's responsible for the big things in your professional life."

He created what he calls his five-minute favor: "Every day, do something selfless for someone else that takes under five minutes. The essence of this thing you do should be that it makes a big difference to the person receiving the gift. Usually these favors take the form of an introduction, reference, feedback, or broadcast on social media."

Adam Grant said, "Adam Rifkin taught me that giving doesn't require becoming Mother Teresa or Mahatma Gandhi; we can all find ways of adding high value to others' lives at a low personal cost. The five-minute favor is my single favorite habit that I learned while writing the book."

What will you do to make giving a part of your connecting strategy?

ACTION

You made it to the end—congratulations! There's still a little work to do, and that includes choosing your three steps and taking action on them today.

Fast Start

One-Hour Win

Snail It

HOUSE LIGHTS UP

I could easily come up with more books for all the information there is to offer on the topic of developing connections. I've shared stories, examples, my strategies, and provided tactics. Ultimately, this all comes back to you because the greatest #connectinghack you have is *you*! Don't just read the book and say, "I'll do it tomorrow." That's when you get stalled and start making excuses. You could meet that one person on your list this week. Are you ready? Is your brand ready? What will you say, and how will you follow up?

It's up to you to take the action items you've been working on from each chapter and plug them into your strategy. There is always the possibility that what you thought it was in chapter one changed based on new information you learned in the book. You may also have a career or life change come up that redefines it again. My goal was to write a book that you can use as a resource on a regular basis. Some of my favorite books are dog-eared and highlighted to the Nth degree. You can do the same with this book to help you refer back as needed, or if you feel you got everything you needed from this book, then consider sharing it with a friend or island alliance who could benefit from it, too. Clean copies are great to give, but so are copies with your handwritten notes inside; each note you write is a way of saying, "Be sure to check this out."

The offer at the beginning of the book holds true. Reach out if you have any questions, would like clarification, are uncertain about a particular tactic, or would even like to share a strategy that's worked for you, by all means let me know. You can do this via social media through Facebook.com/joycelaymanfan or Twitter.com/joycelayman. Of course, email is always an option.

I close my keynotes and workshops with this quotation from Mary Morrissey: "Inspiration without action is merely entertainment." The same holds true for you. This is your chance to take what you learned and apply it to create and maximize your connecting advantage.

To your success!

CURTAIN CALL

Finally, you're invited to join me in the Facebook community for *Your Connecting Advantage*. It's a closed group and requests to join have to be approved. The group is designed to help you find key connections, resources, and information. It's also where you contribute to the discussion and share best practices for connecting. I know business will happen, but I also know some other great things are going to come out of it. I hope to see you there!

www.facebook.com/yourconnectingadvantage

#CONNECTINGHACKS, SHORTCUTS, AND REINVENTING WHEELS

Considering how quickly things change, it would be impossible to list every #connectinghack in Your Connecting Advantage. That would be a full time job in itself. The following are the hacks included in the book, and you can also find the most up-to-date list on my website by going to:

www.yourconnectingadvantage.com/connectinghacks

Business Card Hacks

Business-card apps that capture images of business cards and create contacts in users' phones

CircleBack – Transforms a business card into actionable information
www.circleback.com/scanbizcards

CamCard – Business card reader and manager
www.camcard.com

Communication Hack

Crystal – Empathetic email communication
www.crystalknows.com
• Free and paid versions

Contact Hack

Vcita – Allows website visitors to contact and schedule appointments
www.vcita.com

Customer Relationship Management (CRM) Hacks

Contactually – CRM for business development
www.contactually.com

Insightly – CRM and project management tool
www.insightly.com

Nimble – Social selling and business development CRM
www.nimble.com

HubSpot – CRM for business development
www.hubspot.com

Zoho – CRM for business development
www.zoho.com
• Free trial and paid versions

Email Hacks

Want to know if and when your follow-up email was read? Check these resources out:

Sidekick by Hubspot www.getsidekick.com

Bananatag www.bananatag.com

Intelliverse Email Tracker www.intelliverse.com

Event Hacks

Apps and websites to find out what's going on with social and networking organizations:

MyChamberApp www.mychamberapp.com

Meetup www.meetup.com

Follow-Up Hacks

Eyejot – Follow up and stay connected by sending a video email with Eyejot

www.corp.eyejot.com

- Free and paid versions

XOBNI – If you're a Yahoo user, then check out XOBNI to manage your address book

www.xobni.com

Job Search Hacks

JibberJobber – Helps you keep track of networking relationships as well as jobs you've applied to

www.jibberjobber.com

Personal Brand Monitoring Hacks

Talkwalker Alerts (free) – Provides alerts like Google Alerts

www.talkwalker.com

Social Media Hacks

Commun.*it* – An engagement tool for Twitter and Facebook

www.commun.it

- Free and paid versions

Edgar – Edgar is social media scheduling tool

www.meetedgar.com

- Paid subscription

Rapportive – An addition to your Gmail account for social media insight

www.rapportive.com

Social Media Examiner – World's largest online social media magazine

www.socialmediaexaminer.com

Social Media Keyword Hacks

Twilert – Twitter keyword search tool

www.twilert.com

Thought Leadership Hacks

LinkedIn SlideShare – Content resource and sharing platform

www.slideshare.net

Quora – Question-and-answer website

www.quora.com

Stack Exchange – Question-and-answer site

www.stackexchange.com

Scoop.it – Platform that helps you aggregate and share content. Includes a scheduling feature.

www.scoop.it

Help A Reporter Out (HARO) – Connects journalists with expert news sources

www.helpareporter.com

You can find a more complete list of #connectinghacks at my website:

www.yourconnectingadvantage.com/connectinghacks

FEATURED EXPERTS

Following are the featured experts in the book. To gain complete access to their wisdom, visit their websites and connect on Twitter.

Adam Grant – Professor at Wharton University and recognized as the highest-rated professor in the Wharton MBA program four times. Thought leader and author of *Give and Take.*

Twitter: @AdamMGrant

Website www.giveandtake.com

Bob Burg – Speaker and national best-selling author of books including *Endless Referrals, The Go-Giver, Adversaries into Allies,* and *It's Not About You.*

Twitter: @BobBurg

Website: www.burg.com

Cameron Herold – Business coach to CEO's, mentor, TEDx speaker, and author of *Double Double.*

Twitter: @CameronHerold

Website: www.cameronherold.com

Daniel Pink – Author of five books, including A *Whole New Mind, To Sell Is Human,* and *Drive.* Co-host and co-executive producer of *Crowd Control* on the National Geographic Channel.

Twitter: @DanielPink

Website: www.danpink.com

Dorie Clark – Marketing strategy consultant, keynote speaker, thought leader, and the author of *Reinventing You.*

Twitter: @DorieClark

Website: www.dorieclark.com

Jayson Gaignard – Entrepreneur and author of *Mastermind Dinners* and the top-rated Mastermind Talks Podcast.

Twitter: @JaysonGaignard

Website: www.jaysongaignard.com

Jeff Haden – LinkedIn Influencer, contributing editor for *Inc. Magazine,* speaker, ghostwriter, and author of four books, including *Transform.*

Twitter: @jeff_haden

Website: www.blackbirdinc.com

William Arruda – Brand strategist, speaker, and author of *Career Distinction.*

Twitter: @williamarruda

Website: www.williamarruda.com

LIST OF SOURCES

CHAPTER 1

www.fastcompany.com/28905/brand-called-you

www.eonline.com/news/688861/the-youtube-star-who-surprised-his-wife-with-a-pregnancy-announcement-was-on-ashley-madison

www.reachpersonalbranding.com/

www.forbes.com/sites/jeannemeister/2012/08/14/job-hopping-is-the-new-normal-for-millennials-three-ways-to-prevent-a-human-resource-nightmare/

www.execunet.com/m_releases_content.cfm?id=3349

www.williamarruda.com

www.onlineidcalculator.com

www.thinkwithgoogle.com/articles/b2b-digital-evolution.html

www.forbes.com/sites/deborahsweeney/2011/05/26/babys-1st-url-3-reasons-why-buying-a-domain-name-for-your-child-is-a-good-idea/

www.ebizmba.com/articles/most-popular-websites

www.ebizmba.com/articles/most-popular-websites

www.help.linkedin.com/app/answers/detail/a_id/59

www.sbomag.com/2014/04/how-smbs-meet-customer-demands/

CHAPTER 2

www.dorieclark.com

www.telegraph.co.uk/news/science/science-news/11607315/Humans-have-shorter-attention-span-than-goldfish-thanks-to-smartphones.html

bschool.pepperdine.edu/career-services/content/elevatorspeech.pdf.

CHAPTER 3

www.academicminute.org/2015/06/tiziana-casciaro-university-of-toronto-professional-networking/

www.advisorperspectives.com/articles/2015/03/03/why-networking-makes-you-feel-dirty-new-research-the-mindset-for-effective-networking

www.thepacificinstitute.com/our-approach

www.wsj.com/articles/not-an-introvert-not-an-extrovert-you-may-be-an-ambivert-1438013534

www.yourcoachingbrain.wordpress.com/2013/01/24/shifting-the-brains-negativity-bias/

CHAPTER 4

www.forbes.com/sites/techonomy/2013/11/15/why-zappos-ceo-hsieh-wants-to-enable-more-collisions-in-vegas/

www.telegraph.co.uk/technology/3304496/Be-lucky-its-an-easy-skill-to-learn.html

CHAPTER 5

www.sociallypsyched.org/item/mere-exposure-effect

www.fastcompany.com/3047240/how-to-be-a-success-at-everything/networking-is-over-welcome-sweatworking?utm_source=facebook

www.youtube.com/watch?v=Ks-_Mh1QhMc

www.nytimes.com/2006/09/24/books/chapters/0924-1st-peas.html?pagewanted=all&_r=0

www.inc.com/jeff-haden/10-habits-of-remarkably-polite-people.html

www.brochuremonster.com/brochure-articles/the-etiquette-of-business-cards.php

CHAPTER 6

Grant Cardone - http://www.entrepreneur.com/article/236916

30% stat - http://www.kayakonlinemarketing.com/infographic-best-practices-for-lead-response-management

https://www.siriusdecisions.com/Who-We-Are.aspx

www.marketingdonut.co.uk/marketing/sales/sales-techniques-and-negotiations/why-8-of-sales-people-get-80-of-the-sales

www.businessnewsdaily.com/5389-in-sales-persistence-pays-off.html

CHAPTER 7

fullyfeline.com/about-fully-feline/

btgstudios.com/

www.fastcompany.com/641124/tipping-point-toast

tremendouslifebooks.org/tv/about-being-tremendous

CHAPTER 8

www.washingtonpost.com/wp-dyn/content/article/2008/12/04/AR2008120403537.html

www.eater.com/2013/5/13/6435721/watch-gordon-ramsay-give-up-on-delusional-restaurant-owners-in

www.buzzfeed.com/ryanhatesthis/this-is-the-most-epic-brand-meltdown-on-facebook-ever#.woB2bpb77

CHAPTER 9

www.fastcompany.com/27953/if-your-goal-success-dont-consult-these-gurus

www.ugmconsulting.com/Do%20written%20goals%20really%20make%20a%20difference%20UGM%20Briefing%2026%20Aug%202011.pdf

druckerinstitute.com/peter-druckers-life-and-legacy

www.linkedin.com/pulse/assumptions-questions-princess-bride-joyce-layman?trk=prof-post

SAVO, Techniques of Social Selling: Just Do It!, 2014

www.toprankmarketing.com/newsroom/guide-to-thought leadership/

bigthink.com/videos/thought leadership-101

www.briantracy.com/blog/time-management/plan-ahead-and-increase-productivity/

www.giveandtake.com/#!evaluateyourself/c10x3

www.forbes.com/sites/kareanderson/2013/07/17/pay-it-forward-with-the-five-minute-favor/

Made in the USA
San Bernardino, CA
15 March 2016